200 super salads

200 super salads

hamlyn **all color**

Alice Storey

An Hachette UK company
www.hachette.co.uk

First published in Great Britain in 2009 by Hamlyn,
a division of Octopus Publishing Group Ltd
189 Shaftesbury Avenue, London WC2H 8JY
www.octopusbooks.co.uk
www.octopusbooksusa.com

Distributed in the US by Hachette Book Group USA
237 Park Avenue, New York NY 10017 USA

Distributed in Canada by Canadian Manda Group
165 Dufferin Street, Toronto, Ontario, Canada M6K 3H6

ISBN: 978-0-600-61946-8

A CIP catalog record for this book is available from the
Library of Congress

Printed and bound in China

5 6 7 8 9 10

Standard level spoon measurements are used in all recipes

Ovens should be preheated to the specified temperature.
If using a fan-assisted oven, follow the manufacturer's
instructions for adjusting the time and temperature.

The varieties of cheese used in this book may not always be
strictly vegetarian, but many cheeses are available in
vegetarian form. Always check the label so that you know
what you are buying.

Eggs should be medium unless otherwise stated; choose free-
range if possible and preferably organic. The Food and Drug
Administration advises that eggs should not be consumed
raw. This book contains some dishes made with raw or lightly
cooked eggs. It is prudent for more vulnerable people, such
as pregnant and nursing mothers, invalids, the elderly, babies,
and young children, to avoid uncooked or lightly cooked
dishes made with eggs.

This book includes dishes made with nuts and nut derivatives.
It is advisable for those with known allergic reactions to nuts
and nut derivatives and those who may be potentially
vulnerable to these allergies, such as pregnant and nursing
mothers, invalids, the elderly, babies, and children, to avoid
dishes made with nuts and nut oils. It is also prudent to check
the labels of pre-prepared ingredients for the possible
inclusion of nut derivatives.

contents

introduction

introduction

A salad can be a simple side dish, served to complement a main course of meat or fish, or it can be a meal in itself, whether it is a light lunch or quickly prepared evening meal, or as an impressive and filling main course for a dinner party.

Salads are created from a combination of foods that are limited only by the imagination. The range and variety of salads that can be made are as diverse as the cultures from which they come, whether it is a hearty, mayonnaise-based potato salad or japanese beef & noodle salad. All salads are best made with seasonally available ingredients, and the recipes should, therefore, be adjusted according to the time of year, to what looks best, and to what is readily obtainable in the shops and in your garden.

Salad leaves

There is such a variety of ingredients readily available from countries all over the world that it is possible to experiment with different combinations and to use ingredients that are unusual and exciting. Even the smallest supermarket offers an extraordinary range of lettuces and salad mixes, from common iceberg and romaine lettuces, to baby spinach mix, beet mix, baby leaf and herbs, radicchio, arugula, and watercress to lamb's lettuce, and if you look in gourmet stores you might find

dandelion leaves, chicory, tatsoi, tarvido, sorrel, and many more. Even edible flowers, such as nasturtiums and marigolds, make a pretty addition to salads. You can also easily grow a range of cut-and-come-again salad leaves in even the smallest garden, and it's possible to buy seeds of unusual cabbages and lettuces that are quick to cultivate.

Dressings

Not only can the ingredients in a salad be adapted according to what is available but the range of dressings used to accompany them is almost endless. Overall a salad dressing not only lubricates the salad but also makes it more flavorful and pleasant to eat. Probably the simplest dressing for a salad is vinaigrette, which, at its most basic, is a simple combination of one part acid to three parts oil. The ingredients can be emulsified to make a smooth paste or simply shaken so that they are loosely combined, resulting in a broken vinaigrette. An emulsion is the blending of two unmixable ingredients, and the mixture is stabilized by the addition to mayonnaise of egg yolks, which contain lecithin, or one of the many types of mustard that are now available.

A basic recipe for vinaigrette is given on page 13, but because there are so many wonderful vinegars available you can adapt the recipe to suit the ingredients in the salad and your own personal preferences. Look out for cabernet sauvignon, chardonnay, balsamic, aceto balsamico, white balsamic, rice wine, cider, red and black Chinese, and sherry vinegars, as well as vinegars flavored with different herbs and fruits.

Using the best quality vinegar and oil is extremely important when it comes to making a good salad into a great one, and when you are simply drizzling olive oil over salads, particularly ones that contain tomatoes, use the finest extra virgin olive oil you can find. However, when you are making a vinaigrette you might prefer to use a less strongly flavored, light olive oil, because the strong flavor of extra virgin olive oil can overwhelm the other, less dominant ingredients. If you

make a vinaigrette it will keep for a few days in the refrigerator but remember to shake it vigorously before using so that the oil and vinegar recombine.

It is possible to flavor fairly neutral vinegars, such as white wine vinegar, by adding herbs and spices, including tarragon (see page 14), chili, and rosemary. Many vinaigrette recipes incorporate fruit and vegetables, such as olives (see page 13), orange, lime, lemon, pomegranate, tomatoes, and clementines. Fruit juice is a wonderful supplement for vinegar as long as the sugar in the fruit complements the ingredients of the salad. The acid from both the fruit juice and the vinegar can be useful for making the raw onion that is often included in salads more digestible. If you mix raw onion into the dressing 15 minutes before adding the dressing to the salad the onion will lose its harshness but retain its flavor.

Although vinaigrette dressings are usually quick to make and light and healthy, there are many other wonderful dressings for salads, including richer ones based on creamy cheeses and mayonnaise. Like vinaigrette, mayonnaise is an emulsion, but it contains egg yolks as well as oil and vinegar and, if desired, mustard of some kind. A basic recipe is given on page 12. Mayonnaise is a great base and can be flavored with all types of ingredients, including seeded mustards, capers, lemon, anchovies, horseradish, garlic (when it becomes Aïoli; see page 12), herbs, and cheese. Mayonnaise-based dressings go particularly well with seafood, but they can be adapted to almost any salad, and many of the dressings used with potato salads are based on mayonnaise, including some of the best known ready-made versions, such as Thousand Island Dressing and Ranch Dressing.

Among the other popular creamy dressings are those based on blue cheese (see page 14), but you can adapt the recipe to incorporate other soft cheeses, including goat cheese, according to the ingredients in the salad. Creamy dressings are the perfect accompaniment for classic combinations such

as apples and pears, when the fruits cut through the richness of the dressing and provide a pleasant counterbalance.

Another way to add interesting flavors to dressings is to use one of the different flavored oils that are now available. Among the flavored oils that you can choose from are walnut, hazelnut, chili, garlic, lemon, and herb. It is also easy to make your own flavored oils (see page 15).

Grains, pasta, & legumes

Grains and legumes are a useful addition to salads, transforming them into filling and satisfying meals, and among the interesting legumes and grains you can try are buckwheat, wild rice, kidney beans, cannellini beans, lima beans, chickpeas, couscous, and quinoa. Canned beans are particularly useful, needing neither the lengthy soaking nor the cooking of the dried types.

Pasta and noodles are also useful for adding bulk and a change of texture to a salad. There is a huge range to choose from, and you can enhance your salads with Italian pastas, such as orecchiette, orzo, and penne, or Asian noodles, including vermicelli noodles, rice noodles, egg noodles, soba noodles, and cellophane noodles. Pasta and noodle salads are delicious served both warm and cold, and they make healthy and satisfying meals. For extra crunch you can add croutons to salads. These are now available ready made, but they are quick and easy to make (see page 44). You can use any type of bread you like and flavor it with herbs, different oils, garlic, and cheese. Vary the size of the croutons according to your own preference and the other ingredients of the salad.

Fruit

Fruit salads are, of course, among the most popular and easy to prepare of all desserts, but fruit can be used in savory salads too, providing a welcome—and sometimes unexpected—contrast of flavors and textures. Pears and Parmesan cheese are a classic combination, but other fruits are ideal accompaniments for meat and cheese.

A salad of fresh fruits is usually a refreshing and palate-cleansing end to a meal, especially if the preceding courses have been rich and heavy, but fruit salads can be special with the combination of exotic fruit and unusual flavors, such as black pepper, basil, tarragon, rose water, and balsamic vinegar. Enhance simple fruit salads by the addition of nuts, mascarpone cheese, crème fraîche, yogurt, whipped cream, ice cream, custard, ginger cookies, chocolate, amaretti cookies, and even alcohol.

Salads no longer have to be viewed as the "healthy" option when it comes to planning meals. The recipes that follow suggest some interesting combinations or ingredients, textures, and flavors to whet your appetite and show that a salad can be a regular addition to your menu.

basic recipes

mayonnaise

Serves 6–8
Preparation time 10 minutes

2 egg yolks
2 teaspoons **Dijon mustard**
1–2 tablespoons **white wine vinegar**
1 cup **olive oil**
salt and **pepper**

Put the egg yolks, mustard, 1 tablespoon vinegar, and a little salt and pepper into a large bowl and beat lightly with a balloon whisk to combine. Beating continuously, start adding the olive oil, a few drops at a time, until the sauce starts to thicken. Gradually add the remaining oil in a very thin, steady stream until the mayonnaise is thick and glossy. Don't add the oil too quickly or the mayonnaise might start to separate. If this happens, try beating in 1 tablespoon warm water. If the mixture curdles completely, beat another egg yolk in a separate bowl and gradually beat it into the curdled sauce. Check the seasoning, adding a little more vinegar if the sauce tastes bland. Mayonnaise can be kept, covered, in the refrigerator for up to 2 days.

aïoli

Serves 6–8
Preparation time 10 minutes

2 egg yolks
1 teaspoon **Dijon mustard**
1–2 tablespoons **lemon juice**
2 **garlic cloves**, crushed
good pinch of **cayenne pepper**
1 cup **sunflower oil** or **olive oil**
salt

Put the egg yolks, mustard, 1 tablespoon lemon juice, the garlic, cayenne pepper, and a little oil in a large bowl and beat together lightly to combine. Follow the Mayonnaise recipe (see above) from the second step. Cover and chill until ready to serve.

vinaigrette

Serves 4
Preparation time 10 minutes

1 teaspoon **superfine sugar**
pinch of **powdered mustard**
2 tablespoons **wine vinegar**
4–6 tablespoons **olive oil**
salt and **pepper**

Beat together the sugar and mustard with the vinegar. Add the oil, season to taste with salt and pepper, and mix together thoroughly. Alternatively, put the ingredients in a screw-top jar, replace the lid, and shake well.

olive vinaigrette

Serves 4
Preparation time 10 minutes

1 **garlic clove**, crushed
1–2 pitted **black olives**, finely chopped
2 tablespoons **balsamic vinegar**
2 tablespoons **lime juice**
1 tablespoon **Dijon mustard**

Beat together the garlic and and olives with the vinegar, lime juice, and mustard. Alternatively, put the ingredients in a screw-top jar, replace the lid, and shake well.

low-calorie french dressing

Serves 8
Preparation time 10 minutes

½ small **onion**
6 tablespoons **olive oil**
2 tablespoons **wine vinegar**
½ teaspoon **mustard**
½ tablespoon **superfine sugar**
pinch of **ground coriander**
3 tablespoons chopped **parsley**
salt and **pepper**

Grate the onion. Beat together all the ingredients until thickened. Season to taste with salt and pepper. Alternatively, put the ingredients, including the grated onion, in a screw-top jar, replace the lid, and shake well.

blue cheese dressing

Serves 4
Preparation time 10 minutes

1 teaspoon **superfine sugar**
pinch of **powdered mustard**
2 tablespoons **wine vinegar**
4–6 tablespoons **olive oil**
1 oz **blue cheese**, such as **Roquefort**
salt and **pepper**

Beat together the sugar and mustard with the vinegar. Add the oil and the crumbled cheese, season to taste with salt and pepper, and mix together thoroughly. Alternatively, put the ingredients in a screw-top jar, replace the lid, and shake well.

Combine the lemon zest, vinegar, tarragon, mustard, and sugar in a small bowl and add salt and pepper to taste. Stir to mix, then gradually beat in the oil. Alternatively, mix all the ingredients in a screw-top jar and shake well to combine.

tarragon & lemon dressing

Makes ¼ cup
Preparation time 5 minutes

finely grated zest of 1 **lemon**
2 tablespoons **tarragon vinegar** (see below)
1 tablespoon chopped **tarragon**
¼ teaspoon **Dijon mustard**
pinch of **superfine sugar**
5 tablespoons **olive oil**
salt and **pepper**

tarragon vinegar

Makes 2 cups
Preparation time 5 minutes

2 cups **white wine vinegar**
2 sprigs of **tarragon**

Put the vinegar into a clean glass bottle and add the sprigs of tarragon. Seal and leave for at least 2 days. The flavor will improve with time.

basil-flavored oil

Makes 1¾ cups
Preparation time 15 minutes

bunch of **basil**
1¾ cups **olive oil**

Blanch the basil in boiling water for
30 seconds, then refresh in cold water.
Squeeze out any excess water from the basil
and chop it roughly. Put the basil in a food
processor or blender with the oil and whiz
until smooth. Pour the oil through a fine
sieve into a clean, dry bottle, seal, and leave
overnight, when the sediment will have settled
and you will be left with a bright green,
basil-flavored oil.

mint & yogurt dressing

Makes ½ cup
Preparation time 5 minutes

½ small **cucumber**, peeled
1 tablespoon **olive oil**
4 tablespoons **plain yogurt**
2 tablespoons chopped **mint**
salt and **pepper**

Cut the cucumber in half lengthwise and
remove the seeds with a teaspoon. Finely
chop the flesh. Mix the cucumber with the oil,
yogurt, and chopped mint and season to taste
with salt (if desired) and pepper.

plum sauce

Serves 4
Preparation time 15 minutes
Cooking time 15–18 minutes

8 oz **plums**
⅔ cup **vegetable stock**
5 tablespoons **port** (optional)
1 teaspoon **allspice**
2 teaspoons **soy sauce**
1 tablespoon **cornstarch**

Peel, pit, and roughly chop the plums and
put them in a saucepan with the stock, port
(if used), allspice, and soy sauce. Bring to a
boil and simmer for 10–15 minutes until the
plums are soft. Transfer to a food processor
or blender and whiz until smooth. Return the
plum mixture to the saucepan and stir in the
cornstarch with about 2 tablespoons water to
make a thick sauce. Keep warm until needed.

side salads

endive & baby romaine salad

Serves **4**
Preparation time **10 minutes**

2 **Belgian endive heads**,
  white and red if possible,
  about 6 oz in total
3 **baby romaine lettuce**
  hearts

Dressing
2 oz **Gorgonzola cheese**
1 tablespoon **Worcestershire**
  sauce
2 tablespoons **Mayonnaise**
  (see page 12)
2 tablespoons **sour cream**
3 tablespoons **olive oil**
1 tablespoon **white wine**
  vinegar
2 tablespoons **lemon juice**
salt and **pepper**

Slice the base of the endive heads and the lettuces and carefully remove the individual leaves. Put the leaves in a large salad bowl.

Make the dressing by beating together all the ingredients. Season to taste with salt and pepper.

Add the dressing to the lettuce and endive leaves, toss briefly to mix, and serve.

For Gorgonzola, pecan, & pear salad, prepare the salad leaves in the same way as above. Add ½ cup toasted pecan nuts and 1 finely sliced pear to the endive and lettuce leaves. Toss well. Beat the dressing ingredients as above, toss through the salad, and serve immediately.

coleslaw

Serves **4**

Preparation time **15 minutes, plus standing**

½ **white cabbage**

¼ **red cabbage**

2 **carrots**

1 **red onion**

2 tablespoons roughly chopped **parsley**

Dressing

1¼ cups **Mayonnaise** (see page 12)

1 tablespoon **white wine vinegar**

½ teaspoon **superfine sugar**

salt and **pepper**

Finely shred both cabbages and the carrots and finely slice the onion. Mix the cabbages and carrots in a large salad bowl with the onion and parsley.

Make the dressing by beating the mayonnaise, vinegar, and sugar and season to taste with salt and pepper. Toss the dressing through the cabbage mixture, then let stand for at least 30 minutes before serving.

For apple & radish slaw, add 1 finely sliced red apple and 5 finely sliced radishes to the coleslaw ingredients. Instead of the mayonnaise dressing, beat together 1 teaspoon Dijon mustard, 2 tablespoons white wine vinegar, and 3 tablespoons olive oil. Add the dressing to the salad, cover, and leave in the refrigerator for at least 30 minutes before serving.

arugula, pear, & pecorino salad

Serves **4**
Preparation time **10 minutes**

5 cups **arugula**
2 **pears**
3 oz **pepper pecorino
   cheese**, cut into shavings

Dressing
1 teaspoon **Dijon mustard**
2 tablespoons **cider vinegar**
2 tablespoons **olive oil**
salt and **pepper**

Make the dressing by beating together the mustard,
cider vinegar, and oil. Season to taste with salt
and pepper.

Put the arugula in a large salad bowl. Finely slice the
pear and add it to the arugula. Add the dressing to
the salad and toss carefully to mix.

Layer most of the shavings of the pecorino through
the arugula and pear salad, garnish with the remaining
shavings, and serve.

For arugula, apple, & balsamic salad, combine
5 cups arugula, 1 finely sliced green apple and 3 oz
shaved pecorino cheese in a large salad bowl. Beat
together 2 tablespoons aged balsamic vinegar and
3 tablespoons olive oil. Add the dressing to the salad,
toss carefully to mix, and serve immediately.

green salad

Serves **4–6**
Preparation time **5 minutes**

8 cups **mixed baby leaves
and herbs,** such as
**watercress, frisée (curly-
leaved chicory), arugula,
tatsoi** or **spinach, chives,
parsley,** and **chervil**

Dressing
1 teaspoon **Dijon mustard**
2 tablespoons **chardonnay
vinegar**
4 tablespoons **olive oil**
salt and **pepper**

Make the dressing by beating together the mustard,
vinegar, and oil. Season to taste with salt and pepper.

Put the mixed leaves into a large salad bowl. Carefully
toss the leaves and herbs with the dressing to combine
and serve immediately.

For green salad with crusted goat cheese, mix
together 1½ cups bread crumbs, 2 tablespoons
crushed hazelnuts, 2 tablespoons chopped parsley,
and 1 crushed garlic clove. Season to taste with salt
and pepper. Cut 4 oz goat cheese into rounds, dip
them in flour, then in lightly beaten egg, then in the
bread crumb mixture. Heat 2 tablespoons vegetable
oil in a large skillet over a medium heat and fry the
cheese slices for 3 minutes on each side until golden
and crispy. Drain on paper towels and serve with the
green salad as above.

garden salad

Serves **4**
Preparation time **10 minutes**

½ **cucumber**
8 oz **cherry tomatoes**
5 cups **baby leaf mix**, such as
   **mizuna, baby chard, lollo
   rosso, purslane,** and **oak-
   leaf lettuce**
1 **avocado**
⅓ cup pitted **black olives**

Dressing
1 teaspoon **Dijon mustard**
2 tablespoons **cider vinegar**
3 tablespoons **olive oil**
salt and **pepper**

Peel and slice the cucumber and halve the tomatoes.
Mix the salad leaves with the cucumber and tomatoes
in a large salad bowl. Pit and peel the avocado, cut the
flesh into dice, and add to the bowl with the olives.

Make the dressing by beating together the mustard,
vinegar, and oil. Season to taste with salt and pepper.

Pour the dressing over the salad, toss carefully to
combine, and serve.

For garden salad with broiled chicken, mix together
the grated zest of 1 lemon, 1 tablespoon chopped
parsley, 1 crushed garlic clove, 2 tablespoons olive
oil, and salt and pepper. Coat 2 chicken breasts, each
about 4 oz, in the mixture and place on a foil-lined
baking sheet. Cook under a preheated hot broiler for
3–4 minutes on each side until cooked through. Slice
the chicken breasts and arrange neatly on top of the
garden salad.

zucchini, feta, & mint salad

Serves **4–6**
Preparation time **10 minutes**
Cooking time **10 minutes**

3 **green zucchini**
2 **yellow zucchini**
olive oil
small bunch of **mint**
1½ oz **feta cheese**
salt and **pepper**

Dressing
2 tablespoons **olive oil**
grated **zest** and **juice** of
  1 **lemon**

Slice the zucchini thinly lengthwise into long ribbons. Drizzle with oil and season with salt and pepper. Heat a griddle pan to very hot and grill the zucchini in batches until marked by the griddle on both sides, then place in a large salad bowl.

Make the dressing by beating together the oil and the grated lemon zest and juice. Season to taste with salt the pepper.

Roughly chop the mint, reserving some leaves for garnish. Carefully mix together the zucchini, mint, and dressing. Transfer them to a large salad bowl, then crumble the feta over the top, garnish with the remaining mint leaves, and serve.

For marinated zucchini salad, thinly slice 3 zucchini lengthwise and put them in a nonmetallic bowl with ½ seeded and sliced red chili, 4 tablespoons lemon juice, 1 crushed garlic clove, and 4 tablespoons olive oil. Season to taste with salt and pepper. Allow the salad to marinate, covered, for at least 1 hour. Roughly chop a small bunch of mint, toss with the salad, and serve immediately.

shaved fennel & radish salad

Serves **4–6**
Preparation time **10 minutes**

2 **fennel bulbs**, about
  1 lb 5 oz in total
10 oz **radishes**
2 tablespoons roughly
  chopped **parsley**

Dressing
4 tablespoons **lemon juice**
2 tablespoons **olive oil**
salt and **pepper**

Slice the fennel and radishes as thinly as possible on a mandolin or with a knife, reserving the fennel fronds for garnish. Toss together in a large salad bowl with the parsley.

Make the dressing by beating together the lemon juice and oil. Season to taste with salt and pepper.

Add the dressing to the salad and toss gently to mix. Garnish with the feathery fennel tips and serve.

For pickled fennel salad, mix together 3 tablespoons cider vinegar, 1 tablespoon toasted cumin seeds, and 1¾ cups water in a small saucepan. Bring to a boil and season to taste with salt and pepper. Immediately pour the liquid over 1 lb 5 oz thinly sliced fennel and let cool. Drain the pickled fennel and serve as a side salad or as an accompaniment to broiled fish.

green beans with almonds

Serves **4**
Preparation time
   10 minutes, plus standing
Cooking time **5 minutes**

1 teaspoon **Dijon mustard**
2 tablespoons **white wine
   vinegar**
1 **shallot**, finely chopped
3 tablespoons **olive oil**
1 lb **green beans**
2 tablespoons **toasted
   slivered almonds**

Mix together the mustard and vinegar in a bowl. Add the finely chopped shallot, and let stand for 10 minutes, then beat in the oil.

Trim and blanch the beans, then toss them in the dressing and serve in a salad bowl topped with the slivered almonds.

For green beans with anchovy dressing, put ⅔ cup olive oil into a small, heavy saucepan and add 3 canned anchovies. Cook over a low heat for 5 minutes until the anchovies have softened and broken down. Remove the pan from the heat and allow the dressing to cool to room temperature. Beat in 2 tablespoons white wine vinegar and some cracked black pepper. Toss 1 lb trimmed and blanched green beans in the dressing and serve immediately.

pickled vegetable salad

Serves **4**

Preparation time **20 minutes,
    plus cooling**

Cooking time **20 minutes**

8 small **shallots**

1 small **cauliflower**

1 **red bell pepper**

4 cups **water**

⅔ cup **white wine vinegar**

5 oz **green beans**

5 oz **sugar snap peas**

1½ cups **watercress**

olive oil

salt and **pepper**

Trim the shallots and break the cauliflower into small florets. Core and seed the bell pepper and cut the flesh into ¾ inch squares.

Put the water and vinegar into a heavy saucepan, bring to a boil and add the cauliflower, pepper, and shallots. Return the liquid to a boil and boil for 2 minutes. Take the saucepan off the heat and allow the vegetables to cool in the liquid.

Trim the beans and sugar snap peas and blanch in lightly salted boiling water. Refresh them in cold water and drain.

When the pickling liquid is cool, strain the vegetables and mix them with the beans, peas, and watercress in a large salad bowl. Dress with olive oil, season to taste with salt and pepper, and serve.

For pickled cucumber & chili salad, cut 2 cucumbers in half lengthwise and remove the seeds by running a small teaspoon along the center. Slice the cucumber diagonally and place in a nonmetallic bowl. Add 1 tablespoon finely sliced pickled ginger, 1 seeded and finely sliced red chili, and 5 finely sliced scallions. Put ½ cup sugar, 5 tablespoons rice wine vinegar, and 1¾ cups water in a heavy saucepan and bring to a boil. Allow to cool, then pour the liquid over the cucumbers and let stand for at least 1 hour. The pickled cucumbers will keep for up to one week in a covered container in the refrigerator.

potato salad

Serves **4–6**
Preparation time **10 minutes,**
  plus cooling
Cooking time **15 minutes**

2 lb **new potatoes**
4 oz **bacon**
1 teaspoon **vegetable oil**
6 **scallions**
¾ cup **Mayonnaise**
  (see page 12)
salt and **pepper**

Halve the potatoes and cook in lightly salted boiling water until tender. Rinse under cold water and allow to cool.

Meanwhile, slice the bacon into thin strips. Heat the oil in a skillet and cook the bacon until golden; drain on paper towels and allow to cool. Finely slice the scallions, reserving some for garnish.

Put the potatoes, finely sliced scallions, and bacon in a large salad bowl. Gently stir in the mayonnaise. Season to taste with salt and pepper, garnish with the reserved scallions, and serve.

For blue cheese & walnut potato salad, add 2 oz blue cheese, 2 tablespoons sour cream, and 1 tablespoon lemon juice to ¾ cup mayonnaise and combine well. Mix the dressing through the cooked potatoes together with 2 tablespoons chopped parsley. Garnish with ⅓ cup toasted walnuts and serve.

red cabbage slaw

Serves **4–6**

Preparation time **20 minutes**, plus marinating

1 lb **red cabbage**

1 **red onion**

1 **raw beet**

2 **carrots**

1 **fennel bulb**

2 tablespoons chopped **parsley** or **dill**

½ cup **raisins** or **golden raisins**

Dressing

6 tablespoons **plain yogurt**

1 tablespoon **cider vinegar** or **white wine vinegar**

2 teaspoons **sweet German mustard** or **Dijon mustard**

1 teaspoon **honey**

1 **garlic clove**, crushed

salt and **pepper**

Trim the stalk end of the red cabbage and finely shred the cabbage. Cut the red onion in half and slice it thinly. Peel the beet and carrots and cut them both into thin matchsticks or grate coarsely. Halve the fennel bulb and shred it finely.

Put all the prepared vegetables, chopped parsley or dill, and raisins in a large salad bowl and toss them with your hands to combine well.

Make the dressing. Mix the yogurt with the vinegar, mustard, honey, crushed garlic, a pinch of salt, and plenty of pepper. Pour this dressing over the slaw, mix well, and let marinate for at least 1 hour. Serve the slaw with rye or sourdough bread.

For crunchy chili slaw, finely slice 8 oz white cabbage and 8 oz red cabbage. Cut 1 carrot into thin ribbons with a peeler and thinly slice 1 red onion and 1 fennel bulb. Make a dressing by mixing together 3 tablespoons sweet chili sauce, 1 tablespoon soy sauce, 1 tablespoon barbecue sauce, 2 tablespoons olive oil, and the juice of 2 limes. Toss the salad in the dressing and allow to stand for at least 30 minutes for the flavors to infuse before serving.

arugula & parmesan salad

Serves **4–6**, as a side dish
Preparation time **5 minutes**

5 cups **arugula**
3 tablespoons **finely grated
Parmesan cheese**
1½ oz **Parmesan cheese
shavings**

Dressing
4 tablespoons **lemon juice**
2 tablespoons **olive oil**
½ teaspoon **Dijon mustard**
salt and **pepper**

Make the dressing by beating together the lemon juice, oil, and mustard. Season to taste with salt and pepper.

Put the arugula in a large salad bowl, sprinkle with the Parmesan, and mix lightly. Pour over the dressing and toss to combine. Garnish the salad with the Parmesan shavings and serve.

For arugula salad with chive dressing, blanch a bunch of chives in boiling water for 30 seconds until bright green. Refresh immediately in cold water. Squeeze out all the excess water, roughly chop, and transfer to a blender. Add 3 tablespoons Mayonnaise (see page 12), 1 tablespoon white wine vinegar, and salt and pepper to taste. Blend until smooth, adjusting the consistency with 1 tablespoon warm water if necessary. Mix 5 cups arugula with a thinly sliced fennel bulb, pour over the dressing, toss together, and serve immediately.

light salads

caesar salad

Serves **4–6**

Preparation time **20 minutes**

Cooking time **12 minutes**

1 **romaine lettuce**

2 oz can **anchovy fillets in olive oil**

1 small **white loaf**

⅓ cup **butter**

3 tablespoons **Parmesan cheese shavings**, to garnish

Dressing

5 tablespoons **Mayonnaise** (see page 12)

4–5 tablespoons **water**

1–2 **garlic cloves**

3 tablespoons finely grated **Parmesan cheese**

salt and **pepper**

Make the dressing. Put the mayonnaise in a small bowl and stir in enough of the water to make a thin, pourable sauce. Pound the garlic to a paste with a little coarse sea salt. Add to the mayonnaise with the Parmesan and stir well. Thin with a little more water if necessary so that the sauce remains pourable. Add pepper to taste and set aside.

Tear the lettuce leaves into bite-size pieces and put them into a large salad bowl. Drain the anchovies, chop them into small pieces and sprinkle over the lettuce.

Cut the bread into 1¼ inch thick slices. Discard the crusts. Melt the butter, brush the slices of bread, then cut the bread into 1 inch squares. Brush a baking sheet with a little melted butter and arrange the bread in a single layer, brushing the sides with any remaining butter. Bake in a preheated oven, 400°F, for about 12 minutes or until the croutons are crisp and a deep golden color. Watch the croutons carefully after 8 minutes, because they tend to color quickly toward the end of the cooking time.

Tip the hot croutons into the salad and quickly drizzle the dressing over the top. Sprinkle the Parmesan shavings over the salad and serve immediately.

For cajun chicken Caesar salad, mix 2 teaspoons cajun seasoning with 4 tablespoons olive oil. Rub 4 chicken breasts in the mixture and allow to marinate for 1 hour in the refrigerator. Heat a griddle pan over a medium heat and cook the chicken for 4–5 minutes on each side until cooked through. Allow to rest for 2 minutes, then slice thinly and serve with Caesar Salad.

greek salad

Serves **2**

Preparation time **10–15
minutes**

½ **cucumber**
4 **plum tomatoes**
1 **red bell pepper**
1 **green bell pepper**
½ **red onion**
½ cup **pitted Kalamata olives**
2 oz **feta cheese**, diced

Dressing
4 tablespoons **olive oil**
1 tablespoon chopped
   parsley
salt and **pepper**

Cut the cucumber and tomatoes into ½–¾ inch chunks and put them in a large salad bowl. Cut the flesh from the bell peppers and carefully remove the ribs and the seeds. Cut the pepper flesh into thin strips and put them in the bowl with the cucumbers and tomatoes. Finely slice the red onion and add to the bowl with the olives.

Make the dressing by beating the oil and parsley. Season to taste with salt and pepper.

Pour the dressing over the salad and toss carefully. Transfer to serving bowls, scatter some feta evenly over each bowl and serve.

For Greek salad with garlic pita bread, rub 4 pita breads with a peeled clove of garlic, drizzle with olive oil, season with salt and pepper, and toast in a preheated oven, 375°F, for 4–5 minutes until crisp. Roughly break the pita breads into pieces, about ¾ inch square, and set aside. Prepare the Greek Salad as above, adding 2 tablespoons chopped basil and 2 tablespoons chopped mint. Toss the salad and serve, garnished with the pita bread pieces and a dollop of hummus on each plate.

niçoise salad

Serves **4**
Preparation time **15 minutes**
Cooking time **10–15 minutes**

13 oz small **potatoes**
7 oz **green beans**, trimmed
5 large **plum tomatoes**
2 tablespoons chopped
   parsley, plus extra leaves
   for garnish
⅓ cup **pitted black olives**
2 tablespoons **lemon juice**
2–3 tablespoons **olive oil**
4 large, **soft-poached eggs**
salt and **pepper**

Cook the potatoes in lightly salted boiling water, allow them to cool and halve them. Meanwhile, bring a large saucepan of lightly salted water to a boil, add the trimmed green beans and blanch for 1–2 minutes until bright green and still firm to the touch. Refresh in cold water, drain, and transfer to a large salad bowl.

Core the tomatoes and cut each one into 6 pieces. Add the tomatoes and chopped parsley to the beans with the potatoes, olives, lemon juice, and oil. Season to taste with salt and pepper.

Transfer the salad to serving plates and top each one with a poached egg cut in half and a drizzle of olive oil. Garnish with the reserved parsley leaves and serve.

For tuna niçoise salad, prepare the salad in the same way as the niçoise salad. Drain 6¼ oz canned tuna in olive oil. Flake the fish and toss it through the niçoise salad and serve, topped with a soft-poached egg, if desired.

turkey & avocado salad

Serves **4**
Preparation time **20 minutes**

12 oz cooked **turkey**
1 large **avocado**
punnet of **mustard** and **cress**
3 cups **mixed salad leaves**
½ cup **mixed toasted seeds**,
   such as **pumpkin** and
   sunflower

Dressing
2 tablespoons **apple juice**
2 tablespoons **plain yogurt**
1 teaspoon **honey**
1 teaspoon **wholegrain**
   mustard
salt and **pepper**

Thinly slice the turkey. Peel, pit, and dice the avocado and mix it with the mustard and cress and salad leaves in a large bowl. Add the turkey and toasted seeds and stir to combine.

Make the dressing by beating together the apple juice, yogurt, honey, and mustard. Season to taste with salt and pepper.

Pour the dressing over the salad and toss to coat. Serve the salad with toasted wholegrain rye bread or rolled up in flat breads.

For crab, apple, & avocado salad, prepare the salad in the same way, using 10 oz cooked, fresh white crabmeat instead of the turkey. Cut 1 apple into thin matchsticks and toss with a little lemon juice to stop it from discoloring. Make a dressing by beating 2 tablespoons apple juice with 3 tablespoons olive oil, a squeeze of lemon juice, and 1 finely diced shallot. Season to taste with salt and pepper. Pour the dressing over the salad, stir carefully to mix, and serve.

panzanella salad

Serves **4**
Preparation time **15 minutes**,
   plus standing

1¼ lb large **tomatoes**
1 tablespoon **sea salt**
5 oz **ciabatta bread**
½ **red onion**, finely chopped
handful of **basil leaves**, plus
   extra for garnish
1 tablespoon **red wine
   vinegar**
2 tablespoons **olive oil**
12 **pickled white anchovies**,
   drained
salt and **pepper**

Roughly chop the tomatoes into ¾ inch pieces and put them in a nonmetallic bowl. Sprinkle with the sea salt and let stand for 1 hour.

Remove the crusts from the ciabatta and tear the bread into rough chunks.

Give the tomatoes a good squash with clean hands, then add the bread, onion, basil, vinegar, and oil. Season to taste with salt and pepper. Mix together carefully and transfer to serving plates. Garnish with the drained anchovies and the reserved basil and serve.

For tomato & bean salad, finely slice 1 red onion, cover with 4 tablespoons red wine vinegar and let stand for about 30 minutes. Cut 5 oz ciabatta bread into chunks and place in a roasting pan. Drizzle with olive oil, season with salt and pepper, and add 2 sprigs of thyme. Cook the ciabatta in a preheated oven, 375°F, until golden and crispy. Dice 10 oz tomatoes and put them in a large bowl. Add 13½ oz can cranberry beans, rinsed and drained, 13½ oz can cannellini beans, rinsed and drained, and 1 bunch of chopped basil. Remove the onion from the vinegar, reserving the vinegar, and add to the salad with 12 drained pickled white anchovies. Add 1 teaspoon Dijon mustard to the reserved vinegar and beat in 5 tablespoons olive oil. Season with salt and pepper. Add the dressing to the salad, toss thoroughly, and serve, garnished with the ciabatta croutons.

spring vegetable salad

Serves **4**
Preparation time **10 minutes**
Cooking time **10 minutes**

1⅓ cups fresh or frozen **peas**
7 oz **asparagus**, trimmed
7 oz **sugar snap peas**
2 **zucchini**
1 **fennel bulb**

Dressing
grated **zest** and **juice** of
   1 **lemon**
1 teaspoon **Dijon mustard**
1 teaspoon **honey**
1 tablespoon chopped **flat
   leaf parsley**
1 tablespoon **olive oil**

Put the peas, asparagus, and sugar snap peas in a saucepan of salted boiling water and simmer for 3 minutes. Drain, then refresh under cold running water.

Cut the zucchini into long, thin ribbons and thinly slice the fennel. Transfer all the vegetables to a large salad bowl and mix together.

Make the dressing by beating together the lemon zest and juice, mustard, honey, parsley, and oil in another bowl. Toss the dressing through the vegetables and serve.

For beet dressing, to serve with spring vegetable salad, prepare the vegetables as above and set aside. Finely slice ½ red onion and 1 garlic clove. Heat 2 tablespoons olive oil in a saucepan over a medium heat and gently cook the onion and garlic. Add 4 precooked beets and 6 roughly chopped sun-blushed tomatoes and continue to cook for 3 minutes. When the onions start to brown deglaze the pan with 2 tablespoons balsamic vinegar. Cook for 1 minute, then add ½ cup chicken or vegetable stock. Reduce the stock by a quarter, then let cool. Transfer the stock to a food processor or blender and whiz until smooth. Season with salt and pepper and add up to 2 tablespoons cream until the dressing reaches a drizzling consistency. Drizzle the dressing over the vegetables and serve.

beet & orange salad

Serves **2–4**
Preparation time **15 minutes**
Cooking time **30 minutes**

7 small **beets**
1 teaspoon **cumin seeds**
1 tablespoon **red wine vinegar**
2 **oranges**
1½ cups **watercress**
3 oz **soft goat cheese**
cracked black pepper

Dressing
1 tablespoon **honey**
1 teaspoon **wholegrain mustard**
1½ tablespoons **white wine vinegar**
3 tablespoons **olive oil**
salt and **pepper**

Scrub and trim the beets and put them in a foil-lined roasting pan with the cumin seeds and vinegar and bake in a preheated oven, 375°F, for 30 minutes or until cooked. Check by piercing one with a knife. Allow the beets to cool slightly and then, wearing food-handling gloves, rub off the skin and slice the globes into halves, or quarters if large.

Meanwhile, peel and segment the oranges. Make the dressing by beating the honey, mustard, vinegar, and oil. Season to taste with salt and pepper.

Put the watercress in a bowl with the beets and add the dressing. Mix gently to combine. Arrange the oranges on a plate, top with the salad, and crumble over the cheese. Season with cracked black pepper and serve.

For marinated goat cheese, sun-blushed tomato, & salami salad, in a small plastic container cover 4 oz soft goat cheese with about 1 cup olive oil. Add 2 sliced garlic cloves, 1 piece lemon rind, a sprig of thyme, and 1 tablespoon toasted cumin seeds. Let marinate overnight. Drain the cheese, discarding the marinade, and allow to dry on paper towels. Thinly slice 4 oz salami and place in a large salad bowl with 5 oz drained sun-blushed tomatoes and 3 cups arugula. Crumble 2¼ oz of the goat cheese into the salad. Make the dressing as above and pour over the salad. Toss carefully to combine, crumble the remaining goat cheese over the top, and serve.

cajun potato & shrimp salad

Serves **2**
Preparation time **10 minutes**
Cooking time **15–20 minutes**

10 oz **new potatoes**
1 tablespoon **olive oil**
8 oz **cooked peeled jumbo shrimp**
1 **garlic clove**, crushed
4 **scallions**, finely sliced
2 teaspoons **cajun seasoning**
1 ripe **avocado**
handful of **alfalfa sprouts**
salt

Halve the potatoes and cook them in a large saucepan of lightly salted boiling water for 10–15 minutes or until tender. Drain well.

Heat the oil in a wok or large, nonstick skillet. Add the shrimp, crushed garlic, finely sliced scallions, and cajun seasoning and stir-fry for 2–3 minutes or until the shrimp are hot. Stir in the potatoes and cook for 1 minute. Transfer to a serving dish.

Peel, pit, and dice the avocado and stir into the salad. Top with the alfalfa sprouts and serve.

For cajun chicken wings with potato & avocado salad, mix together 2 tablespoons vegetable oil and 2 teaspoons cajun seasoning. Marinate 12 chicken wings in the mixture for at least 1 hour. Put the chicken wings on a foil-lined baking sheet and cook under a preheated hot broiler for 8–10 minutes until golden and cooked through. Prepare the potatoes as above and stir-fry in a wok or nonstick skillet with 1 crushed garlic clove, 4 sliced scallions, and 2 teaspoons cajun spice. Mix with the avocado and serve with a wedge of lettuce and the chicken wings.

pea & fava bean salad

Serves **4**
Preparation time **15 minutes**
Cooking time **10 minutes**

1 cup frozen **peas**
1 cup **fava beans**
1½ cups **snow pea tendrils**
small bunch of **mint**, roughly
   chopped
5 oz **feta cheese**

Dressing
1 teaspoon **Dijon mustard**
2 tablespoons **olive oil**
1 tablespoon **chardonnay**
   vinegar
salt and **pepper**

Bring a large saucepan of lightly salted water to a boil
and cook the peas for 2 minutes. Refresh in cold water.
Cook the fava beans for 3 minutes, refresh, and peel
to reveal the bright green inside. Mix the peas and
fava beans with the snow pea tendrils and roughly
chopped mint.

Make the dressing by beating the mustard, oil, and
vinegar. Season to taste with salt and pepper.

Crumble the feta into the salad, carefully mix in the
dressing, and serve.

For pea, fava bean, & chorizo salad, prepare the
peas and fava beans in the same way as above. Put
them in a bowl with the snow pea tendrils and add
1 grated zucchini. Thinly slice 3 chorizo sausages
diagonally and fry in a hot skillet until golden and
crispy. Drain on paper towels, then add to the salad.
Beat the dressing ingredients as above and toss the
salad with the mint and feta. Serve immediately.

orange & avocado salad

Serves **4**
Preparation time **20 minutes**

4 large juicy **oranges**
2 small ripe **avocados**
2 teaspoons **cardamom pods**
3 tablespoons **olive oil**
1 tablespoon **honey**
pinch of **allspice**
2 teaspoons **lemon juice**
salt and **pepper**
sprigs of **watercress**,
   to garnish

Cut the skin and the white membrane off the oranges. Working over a bowl to catch the juice, cut between the membranes to remove the segments. Peel and pit the avocados, slice the flesh, and toss gently with the orange segments. Pile onto serving plates.

Reserve a few whole cardamom pods for garnishing. Crush the remainder using a mortar and pestle to extract the seeds or place them in a small bowl and crush with the end of a rolling pin. Pick out and discard the pods.

Mix the seeds with the oil, honey, allspice, and lemon juice. Season to taste with salt and pepper and stir in the reserved orange juice. Garnish the salads with sprigs of watercress and the reserved cardamom pods and serve with the dressing spooned over the top.

For orange, avocado, & honey duck salad, prepare the salad as above. Score 4 duck breasts with a diamond pattern on the fat side of the breast. Place the duck, skin side down, in a large skillet, season with salt and pepper and cook for 5–6 minutes until golden. Turn the duck over, drizzle with honey, and cook for an additional 6 minutes or until cooked through. Set aside and allow to rest for 10 minutes. Slice the duck and serve with the orange and avocado salad.

smoked trout & grape salad

Serves **2**
Preparation time **15 minutes**

7 oz **smoked trout**
1 cup **red seedless grapes**
1½ cups **watercress**
1 **fennel bulb**

Dressing
3 tablespoons **Mayonnaise**
   (see page 12)
4 **cornichons**, finely diced
1½ tablespoons **capers**,
   chopped
2 tablespoons **lemon juice**
salt and **pepper**

Flake the smoked trout into bite-size pieces, removing any bones, and place in a large salad bowl.

Wash and drain the grapes and watercress and add them to the bowl. Finely slice the fennel and add to the mix.

Make the dressing by mixing the mayonnaise, cornichons, capers, and lemon juice. Season to taste with salt and pepper, then carefully mix through the salad and serve.

For crispy trout salad, add 1 finely chopped hard-cooked egg, 2 finely chopped anchovy fillets, and 1 tablespoon chopped parsley to the dressing. Prepare the salad as above, adding 1 green apple, cut into matchsticks. Season 2 pieces of fresh trout, each about 5 oz, with salt and pepper. Heat 1 tablespoon vegetable oil in a skillet over a high heat and cook the trout, skin side down, for 4 minutes, pressing it down with a spatula to give an evenly crispy skin. Turn over the fish and cook for an additional 2 minutes or until it is just cooked through. Remove from the pan. Toss the salad with the dressing and serve immediately with the crispy trout.

watermelon & feta salad

Serves **4**
Preparation time **10 minutes**
Cooking time **2 minutes**

1 tablespoon **black sesame seeds**
1 lb **watermelon**
6 oz **feta cheese**
1¾ lb **arugula**
sprigs of **mint**, **parsley,** and **cilantro**
6 tablespoons **olive oil**
1 tablespoon **orange flower water**
1½ tablespoons **lemon juice**
1 teaspoon **pomegranate syrup** (optional)
½ teaspoon **superfine sugar**
salt and **pepper**

Heat a skillet and dry-fry the sesame seeds for 2 minutes until aromatic, then set aside.

Peel, seed, and dice the watermelon and dice the feta. Arrange the watermelon and feta on a large plate with the arugula and herbs.

Beat together the oil, orange flower water, lemon juice, pomegranate syrup (if used), and sugar. Season to taste with salt and pepper, then drizzle over the salad. Sprinkle with the sesame seeds and serve with toasted pita bread.

For tomato, feta, & basil salad, cut 1½ lb tomatoes into wedges and carefully transfer them to a large salad bowl. Make the dressing by beating together in a small bowl 3 tablespoons aged balsamic vinegar and 6 tablespoons olive oil. Add 1¾ lb arugula, a small handful of basil leaves, and the sprigs of mint and parsley to the tomatoes. Crumble over 6 oz feta cheese, drizzle over the dressing, and combine lightly. Garnish with 3 tablespoons toasted pine nuts and serve.

chicken, apricot, & almond salad

Serves **4**

Preparation time **10 minutes**

8 oz **celery**

½ cup **almonds**

3 tablespoons chopped **parsley**

4 tablespoons **Mayonnaise** (see page 12)

3 poached or roasted **chicken breasts**, each about 5 oz

12 fresh **apricots**

salt and **pepper**

Thinly slice the celery sticks diagonally, reserving the yellow inner leaves. Transfer to a large salad bowl together with half the leaves. Roughly chop the almonds and add half to the bowl with the parsley and mayonnaise. Season to taste with salt and pepper.

Arrange the salad on a serving plate. Shred the chicken and halve and pit the apricots. Add the chicken and apricots to the salad and stir lightly to combine. Garnish with the remaining almonds and celery leaves and serve.

For grilled chicken with apricot & tomato salad,

marinate 4 chicken breasts, each about 5 oz, with 2 crushed garlic cloves, 3 tablespoons sweet chili sauce and the juice and zest of 1 lime for at least 1 hour. Remove the chicken from the marinade and transfer to a heated griddle pan. Cook until golden and cooked through. Remove the pits and chop 12 apricots into ¼ inch pieces. Mix with 3 ripe tomatoes cut into ¼ inch pieces and 2 tablespoons chopped cilantro. Beat together 3 tablespoons red wine vinegar, 3 tablespoons olive oil, 1 teaspoon brown sugar, and 1 teaspoon soy sauce and pour the dressing over the salad. Combine well and serve with the chicken.

daikon, carrot, & red pepper salad

Serves **4**
Preparation time **15 minutes**
Cooking time **2–3 minutes**

1 small **daikon**
3 **carrots**
1 large, firm **red bell pepper**
1 tablespoon **toasted sesame seeds**
1 teaspoon **sesame oil**
1 tablespoon **mirin**
1 tablespoon **rice wine vinegar**
4 **scallions**, finely shredded
cilantro leaves, to garnish

Grate or shred the daikon, carrots, and bell pepper. If the bell pepper proves difficult to shred, thinly slice it into julienne strips. Place the vegetables and the sesame seeds in a bowl and mix together with your hands.

Put the sesame oil, mirin, and vinegar in a small pan and heat gently for 2–3 minutes to blend the flavors. Remove the pan from the heat and allow the mixture to cool a little.

Arrange the salad in a mound in the center of each of 4 plates and pour the dressing over and around it. Top each salad with finely shredded scallions, garnish with cilantro leaves, and serve.

For daikon salad with Asian-style ribs, make a marinade in a small saucepan by combining 5 tablespoons soy sauce, 2 tablespoons brown sugar, 2 tablespoons rice wine vinegar, ½ inch fresh ginger root, peeled and sliced, the zest and juice of 1 orange, 1 cinnamon stick, and 1 star anise. Warm the marinade thoroughly, stirring until the sugar has dissolved, then allow to cool. Cut 1 lb 2 oz pork spare ribs into pieces, pour the marinade over them, and let marinate overnight. Arrange the spare ribs on a foil-lined baking sheet and broil for 20 minutes until sticky, rotating and basting occasionally. Prepare the salad as above and serve with the cooked ribs.

fattoush

Serves **4–6**
Preparation time **15 minutes**
Cooking time **5 minutes**

5 ripe **tomatoes**
1 **cucumber**
1 **green bell pepper**
1 **red bell pepper**
½ **red onion**
4 **flat breads**
2 tablespoons **olive oil**
salt and **pepper**

Dressing
1 **garlic clove**, crushed
4 tablespoons **lemon juice**
3 tablespoons **olive oil**
2 tablespoons chopped
  parsley
2 tablespoons chopped **mint**

Cut the tomatoes, cucumber, green and red bell peppers, and onion into ½ inch pieces and put them in a nonmetallic bowl.

Cut the flat breads into ½ inch squares. Heat the oil in a skillet and fry the bread in batches. Drain on paper towels and allow to cool.

Make the dressing by beating together the garlic, lemon juice, oil, parsley, and mint.

Pour the dressing over the vegetables, toss carefully, and season to taste with salt and pepper. Garnish with the croutons and serve immediately.

For whole grilled sardines with fattoush salad, gut and bone 8 whole sardines and put them on a baking sheet. Put 1 sprig of rosemary in each cavity. Mix together 4 tablespoons olive oil and 1 crushed garlic clove and brush the sardines with the garlic-flavored oil. Season to taste with salt and pepper. Cook the sardines on a barbecue or under a preheated hot broiler for 3 minutes on each side. Remove the sardines from the heat and serve with the fattoush salad and wedges of lemon.

fig, raspberry, & prosciutto salad

Serves **4–6**
Preparation time **5 minutes**

3 cups **arugula and beet
  salad mix**
6 ripe **figs**, halved
1¼ cups **raspberries**
8 slices of **prosciutto**
2 large **buffalo mozzarella
  balls**, each about 5 oz

Dressing
2 tablespoons **aged balsamic
  vinegar**
2 tablespoons **olive oil**

Put the arugula and beet leaves in a large bowl, add
the halved figs, the raspberries, and the prosciutto, toss
carefully and transfer to a large serving plate.

Make the dressing by beating together the vinegar and
oil. Tear each mozzarella ball into 3 pieces and arrange
them on the salad. Drizzle the dressing over the salad
and serve.

For broiled fig & raspberry fruit salad, cut 6 ripe
figs in half and sprinkle ½ tablespoon superfine sugar
over each half. Cook under a preheated hot broiler for
3–4 minutes until golden. Put on a plate with 1¼ cups
raspberries, drizzle with 2 tablespoons balsamic
vinegar, and serve as a dessert.

walnut & blue cheese salad

Serves **4**
Preparation time **15 minutes**
Cooking time **5 minutes**

½ cup **walnut halves**
2 tablespoons **confectioners' sugar**
2 **Belgian endive heads**
1 cup **arugula**
1 **radicchio**, separated into leaves
4 oz **blue cheese**, such as **Roquefort**

Dressing
1 teaspoon **Dijon mustard**
2 tablespoons **cider vinegar**
4 tablespoons **olive oil**

Put the walnuts in a plastic bag with the confectioners' sugar and 1 tablespoon water and shake them until coated. Arrange the nuts on a baking sheet and roast in a preheated oven, 350°F, for 5 minutes or until gold and crusted.

Separate the endive leaves and put them into a large salad bowl with the arugula and radicchio. Crumble over the cheese and add the walnuts. Toss carefully.

Make the dressing by beating together the mustard, vinegar, and oil. Drizzle the dressing over the salad, mix lightly, and serve.

For griddled radicchio & endive salad, cut 2 Belgian endive heads in half and 2 radicchio into quarters. Dust well with about 2 tablespoons confectioners' sugar and place on an oiled griddle over medium heat. Griddle the endive heads and radicchio until golden and caramelized. Combine 3 tablespoons cider vinegar and 4 tablespoons olive oil with 2 tablespoons golden raisins and heat in a small saucepan. Pour over the salad and combine well. Garnish with 3 tablespoons roughly chopped parsley and 4 oz crumbled Gorgonzola cheese.

raspberry salad with toasties

Serves **4**

Preparation time **15 minutes**

Cooking time **4 minutes**

½ **red onion**, thinly sliced

2½ cups **mixed salad leaves**, including **baby red chard leaves**

1 cup fresh **raspberries**

2 tablespoons **balsamic vinegar**

1 **pomegranate**

8 slices, about 3 oz, **whole-wheat French bread**

1 cup **cottage cheese**

little **paprika**

Put the onion in a bowl with the salad leaves and raspberries. Drizzle over the vinegar and toss together.

Cut the pomegranate into quarters, flex the skin, and pop out the seeds. Sprinkle half the seeds over the salad, then transfer the salad to 4 serving plates.

Toast the bread on both sides and arrange 2 slices in the center of each serving plate. Spoon the cottage cheese on to the toast, sprinkle with the remaining pomegranate seeds and a little paprika, and serve.

For raspberry salad dressing, to serve with the above salad, put 1 cup raspberries, 6 tablespoons raspberry vinegar, ⅔ cup olive oil, 1 teaspoon superfine sugar, 1 teaspoon Dijon mustard, 2 tablespoons chopped tarragon, and 1 chopped garlic clove in a food processor or blender. Whiz until smooth, then taste and adjust the seasoning with salt and pepper. If you would like the dressing really smooth pour it through a fine sieve. It will keep, covered, for up to 7 days in the refrigerator.

chop salad, mexican style

Serves **4**
Preparation time **10 minutes**

1 **iceberg lettuce**
13½ oz can **red kidney beans**,
   drained and rinsed
1 **avocado**, peeled, pitted,
   and diced
2 ripe **tomatoes**, chopped
½ **red onion**, finely diced
1 tablespoon chopped
   cilantro leaves
1 **jalapeño chili** (optional),
   finely sliced
corn chips, to garnish
sour cream (optional),
   to serve

Dressing
juice of 1½ **limes**
3 tablespoons **olive oil**

Cut the lettuce into bite-size pieces and put them into a large salad bowl. Add the beans, avocado, tomatoes, and onion with the cilantro and chili (if used). Mix all the ingredients together.

Make the dressing by beating together the lime juice and oil. Drizzle the dressing over the salad and mix lightly to combine. Garnish with lightly crushed corn chips and serve with sour cream (if desired).

For cranberry & chicken chop salad, roughly chop 2 romaine lettuces and put the pieces into a large salad bowl. Shred 3 poached chicken breasts, each about 5 oz, and add to the lettuce with ½ cup toasted pecan nuts, ½ cup dried cranberries, 1 diced red apple, and 1 cored, seeded, and chopped green bell pepper. Beat 2 tablespoons apple cider vinegar with 4 tablespoons olive oil and season to taste with salt and pepper. Drizzle the dressing over the salad and lightly toss to combine. Garnish with crushed plain corn chips and serve.

tomato & mozzarella salad

Serves **4–6**
Preparation time **15 minutes**

1 lb ripe **tomatoes**, preferably
   different types, such as
   heirloom and **cherry**
   and **plum**
about 3 tablespoons **olive oil**
2 tablespoons **aged balsamic**
   vinegar
small handful of **basil leaves**
5 oz **mini mozzarella balls**
salt and **pepper**

Cut half the tomatoes into thick slices and the other half into wedges. Arrange the slices on a large serving plate, slightly overlapping each other.

Put the tomato wedges into a bowl and drizzle with olive oil and balsamic vinegar. Season to taste with salt and pepper. Mix carefully and arrange on top of the tomato slices.

Add the basil leaves and mozzarella balls to the tomato wedges. Drizzle the salad with more olive oil and balsamic vinegar, season to taste with salt and pepper, and serve.

For tomato & pasta salad, cook 8 oz fusilli or penne until it is just tender. Refresh in cold water. Chop 1 lb tomatoes into chunks and stir through the still warm pasta, coat with olive oil, and season to taste with salt and pepper. Mix through a large handful of torn basil leaves, garnish with Parmesan cheese shavings, and serve.

big salads

thai-style beef salad

Serves **4–6**
Preparation time **20 minutes**
Cooking time **10 minutes**

4 oz **green papaya**, peeled
   and seeded
4 oz **green mango**, peeled
   and pitted
handful of **mint leaves**
handful of **Thai basil leaves**
2 small, **elongated shallots**
1 tablespoon **vegetable oil**
4 **sirloin steaks**, each about
   4 oz

Dressing
½ **chili**, seeded
½ inch **fresh ginger root**,
   peeled and finely sliced
1½ tablespoons **palm sugar**
juice of 2 **limes**
2 tablespoons **Thai fish
   sauce** (nam pla)

Finely grate or slice the papaya and mango into long, thin strips. Combine the mint and basil leaves in a large salad bowl with the mango and papaya. Finely slice the shallots and add them to the mixture.

Make the dressing. Crush the chili with the ginger and sugar using a mortar and pestle. Add the lime juice and fish sauce to taste.

Heat a griddle pan on a high heat, add the oil, and fry the steak for 5 minutes on each side. Remove the steak from the pan and allow it to rest for 5 minutes.

Thinly slice the steak diagonally and arrange neatly on the serving plates. Add the dressing to the salad, mix well to combine, and serve with the steak.

For toasted rice khao koor, a special garnish you can add to this salad, put 3 tablespoons raw jasmine rice in a small skillet over a medium heat and continue stirring until all the rice is golden in color. Allow the rice to cool, then grind it coarsely in a spice grinder or using a mortar and pestle, and sprinkle over the finished salad.

spiced chicken & mango salad

Serves **4**

Preparation time **15 minutes**

Cooking time **5 minutes**

4 boneless, skinless **chicken breasts**, about 5 oz each

6 teaspoons **mild curry paste**

4 tablespoons **lemon juice**

⅔ cup **plain yogurt**

1 **mango**, peeled, pitted, and cut into chunks

1 cup **watercress**

½ **cucumber**, diced

½ **red onion**, finely chopped

½ **iceberg lettuce**

Cut the chicken breasts into long, thin slices. Put 4 teaspoons of the curry paste in a plastic bag with the lemon juice and mix together by squeezing the bag. Add the chicken and toss together.

Half-fill the base of a steamer with water and bring to a boil. Steam the chicken in a single layer, covered, for 5 minutes until cooked. Test with a knife or metal skewer; the juices will run clear when it is done.

Meanwhile, mix the remaining curry paste in a bowl with the yogurt.

Tear the watercress into bite-size pieces. Add it to the yogurt dressing with the cucumber, red onion, and mango and toss gently.

Tear the lettuce into pieces and arrange on 4 plates. Spoon the mango mixture over the top, add the warm chicken strips, and serve immediately.

For chili shrimp, mango, & avocado salad, replace the chicken with 13 oz peeled, raw jumbo shrimp with the tails on. Prepare the salad in the same way as above but add the diced flesh of an avocado. Heat 2 tablespoons vegetable or peanut oil in a nonstick skillet over a high heat, and fry 1 finely chopped red chili for 1 minute, then add the shrimp and 2 finely chopped garlic cloves. Fry for 2 minutes until the shrimp are pink and just cooked through. Mix through the salad and serve immediately.

japanese beef & noodle salad

Serves **4**

Preparation time **15 minutes**, plus marinating

Cooking time **15 minutes**

2 **sirloin steaks**, each about 8 oz

5 oz **soba noodles**

1 small **daikon**, peeled and finely sliced

2 **carrots**, peeled and finely sliced

½ **cucumber**, peeled and finely sliced

Dressing

1 **garlic clove**, finely chopped

¾ inch **fresh ginger root**, peeled and chopped

5 tablespoons **soy sauce**

4 tablespoons **sweet chili sauce**

5 teaspoons **sesame oil**

To garnish

5 **scallions**, finely sliced

2 tablespoons **toasted sesame seeds**

Make the dressing. Mix the garlic and ginger with the soy sauce, sweet chili sauce, and sesame oil. Put the steaks in a nonmetallic dish and add 2 tablespoons of the dressing, reserving the rest. Cover and let marinate for at least 2 hours, or preferably overnight.

Bring a saucepan of lightly salted water to a boil and cook the noodles for about 5 minutes or until done. Refresh in cold water, drain, and transfer to a bowl.

Add the vegetables to the bowl with the noodles.

Heat a griddle pan on a high heat and cook the steaks for 5 minutes on each side until medium rare (longer if you prefer your meat well done). Allow to rest for 5 minutes and then finely slice. Drizzle the dressing over the noodle and vegetable mixture, add the sliced steak, and combine well. Garnish with scallions and toasted sesame seeds and serve immediately.

For sesame-crusted salmon & soba noodle salad, combine 1 tablespoon black sesame seeds, 1 tablespoon white sesame seeds, and 1 tablespoon coriander seeds. Put 4 small fillets of salmon, each about 4 oz, flesh side down into the seed mix and press the seeds onto the flesh. Heat 1 tablespoon vegetable oil in a large skillet over a medium heat and fry the salmon, flesh side down, for 1 minute. Turn over the salmon and fry for about 4 minutes or until the salmon is just cooked through. Serve with the noodle salad as above, garnished with cilantro leaves.

italian broccoli & egg salad

Serves **4**
Preparation time **10 minutes**
Cooking time **8 minutes**

4 **eggs**
10 oz **broccoli**
2 small **leeks**, about 10 oz
   in total
sprigs of **tarragon**, to garnish
   (optional)

Dressing
4 tablespoons **lemon juice**
2 tablespoons **olive oil**
2 teaspoons **honey**
1 tablespoon **capers**, drained
2 tablespoons chopped
   tarragon
salt and **pepper**

Half-fill the base of a steamer with water, add the eggs, and bring to a boil. Cover with the steamer top and simmer for 8 minutes or until hard-cooked.

Meanwhile, cut the broccoli into florets and thickly slice the stems. Trim, slit, and wash the leeks and cut them into thick slices. Add the broccoli to the top of the steamer and cook for 3 minutes, then add the leeks and cook for an additional 2 minutes.

Make the dressing by mixing together the lemon juice, oil, honey, capers, and tarragon in a salad bowl. Season to taste with salt and pepper.

Crack the eggs, cool them quickly under cold running water, and remove the shells. Roughly chop the eggs.

Add the broccoli and leeks to the dressing, toss together, and add the chopped eggs. Garnish with sprigs of tarragon (if desired) and serve warm with thickly sliced whole-wheat bread.

For broccoli, bacon, & pine nut salad, cut 4 oz pancetta into pieces about ¼–1¼ inches. Heat a pan and dry-fry the pancetta until golden and crispy, then drain on kitchen paper. Toast 4 tablespoons pine nuts in a dry pan over a low heat until golden and toasted. Mix the pancetta with the broccoli and leeks, make a dressing as above, and serve sprinkled with the pine nuts instead of the eggs.

bang bang chicken salad

Serves **4**
Preparation time **15 minutes**
Cooking time **10 minutes**

2 oz **dried vermicelli noodles**
¼ **Savoy cabbage**, finely
  shredded
1 **carrot**, finely chopped
½ **cucumber**, finely chopped
juice of 1 **lime**
½ cup **peanut butter**
3 tablespoons **sweet chili**
  sauce
1 tablespoon **soy sauce**
1 teaspoon **Chinese vinegar**
2 tablespoons **sesame oil**
2 tablespoons **vegetable oil**
3 poached **chicken breasts**,
  each about 5 oz
3 finely sliced **scallions**,
  to garnish

Bring a large saucepan of water to a boil and cook the noodles for 2 minutes. Refresh in cold water, drain, and transfer to a large salad bowl.

Add the cabbage, carrot, cucumber, and lime juice to the noodles.

Gently warm the peanut butter in a small saucepan. Add the sweet chili sauce, soy sauce, vinegar, and sesame and vegetable oils and beat to a pouring consistency. (If necessary, add a little warm water to achieve the correct consistency.) Set the sauce aside to cool slightly.

Shred the chicken breasts, add the meat to the noodle mix and combine well. Arrange on serving plates, spoon over the peanut sauce, and garnish with finely sliced scallions.

For spicy beef skewers with noodle salad, cut 1 lb 10 oz sirloin steak into ¾ inch squares. Mix together 1 tablespoon each ground ginger, chopped cilantro, and crushed cumin seeds with 3 crushed garlic cloves, 1 teaspoon dried red pepper flakes, and about ¼ cup olive oil. Cover the beef in the mixture and let marinate for at least 1 hour. Thread the beef onto metal or presoaked wooden skewers and cook on a barbecue or a preheated hot griddle pan for 3 minutes on each side until cooked through. Serve with the noodle salad and spoon over the dressing.

mango & smoked chicken salad

Serves **4**

Preparation time **15 minutes**

2 ripe **avocados**, halved,
   pitted, and peeled
2 tablespoons **lemon juice**
1 small **mango**
handful of **watercress**
¼ cup finely sliced **cooked
   beets**
6 oz **smoked chicken**

Dressing
3 tablespoons **olive oil**
1 teaspoon **wholegrain
   mustard**
1 teaspoon **honey**
2 teaspoons **cider vinegar**
salt and **pepper**

Slice or dice the avocado flesh and put it in a shallow bowl with the lemon juice.

Cut the mango in half on either side of the central pit, peel away the skin, and slice or dice the flesh.

Make the dressing. Beat together the oil, mustard, honey, and vinegar. Season to taste with salt and pepper. Remove the avocado from the lemon juice and mix the juice into the dressing.

Arrange the watercress and beets on 4 plates or in a salad bowl and add the avocado and mango. Drizzle the dressing over the salad and stir to combine. Thinly slice the chicken and top the salad with the meat. Serve immediately.

For smoked chicken, white bean, & thyme salad,
rinse and drain 2 x 13½ oz cans cannellini beans and mix with 8 oz halved cherry tomatoes, 2 cups arugula, ⅓ cup pitted green olives, and 1 tablespoon chopped thyme. Make the dressing by beating 1 teaspoon Dijon mustard, 2 tablespoons cider vinegar, 4 tablespoons olive oil, and 1 tablespoon chopped thyme. Dress the salad and serve with 6 oz thinly sliced smoked chicken.

duck, clementine, & tatsoi salad

Serves **4–6**
Preparation time **20 minutes**
Cooking time **15 minutes**

3 **duck breasts**, each about
  8 oz
10 oz **green beans**, trimmed
3 **clementines**, peeled and
  segmented
4 cups **tatsoi** or **spinach**

Dressing
juice of 2 **clementines**
1 tablespoon **white wine
  vinegar**
4 tablespoons **olive oil**
salt and **pepper**

Put the duck breasts, skin side down, in a cold ovenproof dish and cook over a medium heat for 6 minutes or until the skin has turned crisp and brown. Turn them over and cook for an additional 2 minutes. Transfer the duck to a preheated oven, 350°F, and cook for 5 minutes until cooked through. Remove the duck breasts from the oven, cover with foil, and let rest.

Meanwhile, blanch the green beans in lightly salted boiling water for 2 minutes until cooked but still firm and bright green. Drain and refresh in cold water. Transfer the beans to a large salad bowl with the clementine segments.

Make the dressing by beating together the clementine juice, vinegar, and oil in a small bowl. Season to taste with salt and pepper.

Add the tatsoi or spinach to the beans and clementines, drizzle over the dressing and combine well. Slice the duck meat, combine it with the salad, and serve immediately.

For orange & mustard dressing, an alternative dressing for this salad, cut 2 oranges in half and place them, flesh side down, on a hot griddle pan. Cook until they are charred and golden. Squeeze the orange juice into a small saucepan and reduce over a medium heat for 5 minutes until slightly thickened. Beat in 1 tablespoon wholegrain mustard and 4 tablespoons olive oil. Allow to cool slightly and serve warm.

prickly pear & prosciutto salad

Serves **4**
Preparation time **15 minutes**

4 **prickly pears**
4 oz **haloumi cheese**
4 slices of **prosciutto**
1 cup **watercress** or **mizuna leaves**
1 large **red chili**, seeded and finely chopped
2 tablespoons **lime juice**
2 tablespoons **pitted black olives**
handful of **chervil** sprigs
salt and **pepper**

Dressing
2 tablespoons **olive oil**
1 tablespoon **orange juice**
1 tablespoon **sherry vinegar**
pinch of **dried red pepper flakes**

Wearing plastic gloves, cut each of the prickly pears in half and then into quarters. Remove the skins if preferred, taking care with the small, hairy spikes.

Thickly slice the haloumi and put one-quarter in the center of each serving plate. Arrange the prosciutto and prickly pear on top of the haloumi with the watercress or mizuna. Sprinkle the chili over the plates with salt and pepper and the lime juice. Sprinkle olives around the plate and add the chervil.

Make the dressing by mixing the oil, orange juice, vinegar, and pepper flakes. Just before serving, drizzle a little of the dressing over the salad and serve at once.

For pear, bresaola, & dolcelatte salad, arrange about 13 oz thinly sliced bresaola on a large serving plate so that the slices are slightly overlapping. Finely slice 2 pears and toss with 3 cups arugula. Arrange the pears and arugula on the bresaola and drizzle with balsamic vinegar and olive oil. Crumble over 4 oz of dolcelatte cheese and serve.

shrimp, mango, & avocado salad

Serves **4**
Preparation time **10 minutes**

1 large **mango**, about 15 oz,
   peeled and pitted
1 ripe **avocado**, about 13 oz,
   peeled and pitted
2 large **romaine lettuces**
16 large **cooked jumbo
   shrimp**, peeled but tails
   left on

Dressing
juice of 2 **limes**
1 teaspoon **palm sugar**
2 tablespoon **vegetable oil**
½ **chili**, seeded and finely
   chopped

Cut the mango and avocado flesh into ¾ inch pieces. Discard the outer layer of leaves and cut the stems off the lettuces, leaving the hearts. Separate the leaves and add them to the mango and avocado with the shrimp.

Make the dressing by beating together the lime juice, sugar, and oil with the chili. Add the dressing to the salad, toss carefully to mix, and serve immediately.

For creamy mayonnaise dressing, a more luxurious accompaniment for this salad, mix 3 tablespoons Mayonnaise (see page 12), 2 tablespoons heavy cream, 2 teaspoons tomato ketchup, 1½ teaspoons Worcestershire sauce, 2–3 drops Tabasco sauce, 1 tablespoon lemon juice, and 1 tablespoon brandy. Season to taste with salt and pepper. Spoon the dressing over the salad or put a spoonful on the side of each plate as a dip for the shrimp.

sesame-crusted salmon salad

Serves **4**
Preparation time **25 minutes**
Cooking time **4–10 minutes**

4 **scallions**
2 **egg whites**
1 tablespoon **white sesame seeds**
1 tablespoon **black sesame seeds**
1 lb **salmon fillet**
1 **frisée (curly-leaved chicory)**, divided into leaves
2 bunches of **watercress**
salt and **pepper**

Dressing
3 tablespoons **white wine vinegar**
5 tablespoons **vegetable oil**
1 tablespoon **sesame oil**
1 tablespoon **soy sauce**
1 teaspoon **superfine sugar**
bunch of **chives**, finely chopped

Cut the scallions into thin strips and put them in cold water.

Lightly beat the egg whites. Mix the white and black sesame seeds with salt and pepper on a large plate. Dip the salmon fillet in the egg whites then roll it in the sesame seeds. Pat the salmon on the seeds all over to give a good, even coating. Heat a griddle pan, add the salmon, and cook for 2 minutes each side for rare or 5 minutes for well done.

Make the dressing by mixing together the vinegar, oils, soy sauce, superfine sugar, and chives. Toss the frisée leaves and watercress in the dressing. Arrange the leaves on a large serving dish.

Finely slice the salmon fillet and place on top of the salad. Drain the scallion curls, dry them on paper towels, and sprinkle over the salmon. Serve immediately.

For sashimi salmon salad, grate 1 raw beet and 2 carrots and mix with 2 cups arugula. Make the dressing as above. Mix together 1 tablespoon each white and black sesame seeds. Slice as thinly as possible 2 skinless fillets of fresh salmon, each 5 oz, and arrange on individual plates. Drizzle the dressing over the salad, garnish with the sesame seeds, and serve with the salmon.

pork larb

Serves **4**

Preparation time **15 minutes**

Cooking time **15 minutes**

1 tablespoon **peanut oil**

¾ inch **fresh ginger root**, peeled and finely chopped

1 **red chili**, seeded and finely chopped

2 **lemon grass stalks**, white stems chopped

3 **kaffir lime leaves**, finely sliced

1¼ lb **ground pork**

2 tablespoons **Thai fish sauce** (nam pla)

juice of 1½ **limes**

1 **iceberg lettuce**

½ **cucumber**

To garnish

3 tablespoons chopped **roasted peanuts**

small bunch of **mint**, finely chopped

small bunch of **cilantro**, finely chopped

Heat the oil in a large, nonstick skillet or wok over a high heat, add the ginger, chili, lemon grass, and lime leaves and fry for 1 minute.

Add the pork and stir-fry for 4–5 minutes until slightly browned and cooked through. Add the fish sauce and lime juice to taste then remove the pan from the heat.

Cut the lettuce into small wedges and the cucumber into batons. Arrange the lettuce and cucumber on serving plates. Serve the pork with the salad, garnished with the chopped peanuts and herbs.

For sang choy bow, instead of cutting the iceberg lettuce into wedges break the leaves into cup shapes. Cook the pork in the same way as above and spoon the mixture into the lettuce leaf cups. Garnish with 3 tablespoons chopped peanuts and mint and cilantro leaves and serve immediately.

peanut, squid, & noodle salad

Serves **4**

Preparation time **25 minutes,** plus standing

Cooking time **15 minutes**

6 oz **thin rice noodles**

1 lb prepared **baby squid**

3 **red chilies,** seeded and finely chopped

3 **garlic cloves,** crushed

2 tablespoons chopped **cilantro,** plus extra leaves to serve

3 tablespoons **peanut oil**

¾ cup **peanuts**

4 oz **green beans,** shredded

3 tablespoons **Thai fish sauce** (nam pla)

1 teaspoon **superfine sugar**

3 tablespoons **lemon juice**

thick **lime wedges,** to serve (optional)

Soak the noodles in boiling water for 5–8 minutes or until they are soft. Drain well and rinse in cold water.

Cut the squid bodies in half lengthwise and make a series of slashes in a diagonal criss-cross pattern on the underside of each piece of squid.

Mix the chilies with the garlic and cilantro. Toss with the squid pieces, then let stand for 20 minutes.

Heat the oil in a wok and toast the peanuts for 2–3 minutes until golden brown. Remove from the oil and reserve. Add the squid to the oil and quickly stir-fry for 2–3 minutes or until they have begun to curl and turn white. Set aside with the peanuts.

Stir-fry the beans for 2 minutes. Mix the fish sauce, sugar, lemon juice, and 3 tablespoons water and cook for an additional 1 minute. Remove the pan from the heat, add the drained noodles and toss together. Add the peanuts, squid, and cilantro leaves and toss again. Serve warm or cool with thick lime wedges, if desired.

For sweet chili & lime chicken, prepare the noodle salad as above but omit the squid and add the chili, garlic, and cilantro to the salad at the end, when tossing. Mix 3 tablespoons sweet chili sauce and the zest and juice of 1 lime. Brush 4 chicken breasts, each about 5 oz, with some of the mixture. Put the chicken, skin side up, on a foil-lined baking sheet and cook under a preheated hot broiler for 8–10 minutes. Brush the chicken again with more of the mixture and cook for 5 minutes until crispy and cooked through. Slice the chicken and serve on top of the salad.

marinated tofu & mushroom salad

Serves **4**

Preparation time **15 minutes**,
plus marinating

Cooking time **5 minutes**

8 oz **firm tofu**

1 lb **mushrooms**, including
enoki, shiitake, wood ear,
and **oyster**

Marinade

1 **garlic clove**, finely chopped

¾ inch **fresh ginger root**,
peeled and finely sliced

5 tablespoons **soy sauce**

1 tablespoon **mirin**

2 tablespoons **sweet chili
sauce**

1½ tablespoons **sesame oil**

2 **star anise**

To garnish

5 **scallions**, finely sliced

2 tablespoons **toasted
sesame seeds**

Make the marinade. Mix the garlic and ginger with the soy sauce, mirin, sweet chili sauce, and oil. Add the star anise. Put the tofu in a nonmetallic dish, pour over the marinade, cover, and refrigerate for at least 2 hours or overnight if possible.

Cut the mushrooms into bite-size pieces and sauté in a hot saucepan for 1 minute. Cut the marinated tofu into ¾ inch squares, mix with the mushrooms, and pour over the remaining marinade. Garnish with finely sliced scallions and sesame seeds and serve immediately.

For tofu & rice salad, cook 1 cup sushi rice according to the instructions on the package. While the rice is still warm season it with ½–⅔ cup sushi pickle. Cut 1 lb mixed mushrooms into bite-size pieces and cook briefly, then mix though the rice with 1 carrot cut into julienne strips and a small bunch of finely sliced scallions. Mix the salad well, garnish with finely sliced deep-fried bean curd and toasted sesame seeds, and serve immediately.

duck, hazelnut, & peach salad

Serves **4**

Preparation time **15 minutes**

Cooking time **20 minutes**

3 **duck breasts**, each about
7 oz

4 **peaches**

6 tablespoons roughly
chopped **toasted hazelnuts**

2½ cups **arugula**

Dressing

1 teaspoon **Dijon mustard**

2 tablespoon **balsamic
vinegar**

4 tablespoons **hazelnut oil**

salt and **pepper**

Heat a griddle pan until it is very hot and fry the duck, skin side down, for 4 minutes or until golden brown. Turn the duck over and cook for 2 minutes, then transfer it to a preheated oven, 375°F, and cook for 6–8 minutes until cooked through. Remove from the oven, cover with foil, and let rest.

Meanwhile, halve the peaches and remove the pits. Heat a griddle pan to a medium heat, add the peach halves, cut side down, and cook until they are golden yellow. Cut the peaches into wedges and mix them in a bowl with the hazelnuts and arugula.

Make the dressing by beating together the mustard, vinegar, and oil. Season to taste with salt and pepper.

Thinly slice the duck meat and add it to the salad. Drizzle over the dressing, combine gently, and serve.

For duck, asparagus, & hazelnut salad, put 4 duck legs on a baking sheet and season with salt and pepper. Roast the duck legs in a preheated oven, 325°F, for 45–60 minutes or until cooked through but not dry. Remove the woody ends from a large bunch of asparagus and transfer the spears to a baking sheet. Cook under a preheated hot broiler for 3–4 minutes, turning occasionally. Remove the asparagus from the broiler and place in a bowl with 6 tablespoons roughly chopped roasted hazelnuts and 2½ cups arugula. Pour over the dressing as above and stir to combine. Serve with the duck.

quail, plum, & cashew nut salad

Serves **4**
Preparation time **20 minutes**
Cooking time **12 minutes**

4 **quails**, butterflied
2 tablespoons **Plum Sauce**
  (see page 15)
4 **plums**, quartered and pitted
2 cups **lamb's lettuce**
⅓ cup **toasted cashew nuts**

Dressing
1 **red chili**, seeded and finely
  chopped
1½ tablespoons **plum sauce**
juice of 1½ **limes**
2 tablespoons **sunflower oil**

Put the quails in a foil-lined baking pan and brush each with some plum sauce. Cook under a preheated hot broiler for 5–6 minutes on each side until golden and just cooked through. Cut each quail into 4 equal sections and place them in a large salad bowl.

Meanwhile, make the dressing by mixing together the chili, plum sauce, lime juice, and oil.

Put the plums, lamb's lettuce, and cashew nuts in the bowl with the quail pieces. Add the dressing, toss lightly to combine, and serve immediately.

For crispy soy quail & pear salad, seed and finely chop 1 red chili and mix it in a bowl with 6 tablespoons soy sauce, 2 tablespoons brown sugar, and the juice and zest of 1 orange. Peel and roughly chop ½ inch fresh ginger root and add to the bowl with 1 star anise. Marinate 4 butterflied quails in the mixture overnight. Slice 2 pears and place them in a large salad bowl with 2 cups lamb's lettuce and 1 finely sliced red bell pepper. Remove the quail from the marinade, arrange them on a foil-lined baking sheet, and cook under a preheated hot broiler for 4 minutes on each side until cooked and crispy. Season with salt and pepper. Toss the salad with the same dressing as above and serve garnished with ⅓ cup toasted cashew nuts.

chicken & asparagus salad

Serves **2**
Preparation time **10 minutes**
Cooking time **5 minutes**

5 oz **asparagus**, cut into
  2 inch lengths
7 oz **smoked chicken breast**
4 oz **cherry tomatoes**, halved
10 oz can **cannellini beans**,
  drained and rinsed
handful of **chives**, chopped

Dressing
2 tablespoons **olive oil**
2 teaspoons **honey**
2 teaspoons **balsamic
  vinegar**
2 teaspoons **wholegrain
  mustard**
1 **garlic clove**

Cook the asparagus in a large saucepan of lightly salted boiling water for about 4 minutes or until just tender. Drain and plunge into cold water to prevent further cooking. Pat dry with paper towels.

Cut the chicken into bite-size pieces and transfer them to a large salad bowl. Add the tomatoes, beans, asparagus, and chopped chives and mix well.

Make the dressing by beating the oil, honey, vinegar, and mustard with the crushed garlic in a small bowl. Pour the dressing over the salad and toss well to coat.

For chicken, asparagus, & haloumi salad,

prepare 5 oz asparagus as above and set aside. Heat a griddle pan and cook 4 chicken breasts, each about 5 oz, for 5–6 minutes on each side or until cooked. Set aside, cover with foil, and keep warm. Cut 8 oz haloumi cheese into ¼ inch slices and fry for 2 minutes on each side until golden and crispy. Mix 1 teaspoon Dijon mustard, 3 tablespoons lemon juice, 4 tablespoons olive oil, and 2 tablespoons roughly chopped tarragon in a small bowl. Slice the chicken and arrange on serving plates with the haloumi and asparagus. Drizzle over the dressing and serve.

duck & soybean salad

Serves **4**
Preparation time **10 minutes**

1 lb **Peking duck**
1 cup cooked **soybeans**
1 **cucumber**
5 **scallions**
Sichuan pepper, to garnish

Dressing
2 tablespoons **hoisin sauce**
4 tablespoons **soy sauce**
juice of **1 lime**

Shred the duck and mix it with the soybeans in a large salad bowl. Cut the cucumber into 1¼ inch batons and finely slice the scallions, reserving some for garnish. Add the cucumber and scallions to the duck mixture.

Make the dressing by beating the hoisin and soy sauces with the lime juice in a small bowl. Drizzle the mixture over the duck salad and toss gently to combine. Garnish with the reserved scallion and a sprinkling of Sichuan pepper and serve at once.

For poached salmon & soybean salad, blanch 10 oz green beans, 1⅓ cups green peas, and 1 cup soybeans in lightly salted boiling water. Refresh in cold water and set aside. Bring a saucepan of lightly salted water to a boil. Put 3 boneless, skinless salmon fillets, each about 6 oz, into the water. Reduce the heat to a rolling simmer and cook for 3–4 minutes until the salmon is still pink in the middle. Remove them from the water and let cool. Cut ½ cucumber into small dice and mix with the blanched vegetables and 1½ cups arugula. Flake the salmon into the vegetables. Beat 2 tablespoons sweet chili sauce, 2 tablespoons soy sauce, and the juice of 1 lime. Drizzle the dressing over the salad and serve immediately.

peanut, pomelo, & shrimp salad

Serves **4**

Preparation time **15 minutes**

Cooking time **1-2 minutes**

1 large **pomelo**

½ cup **peanuts**, toasted and
roughly chopped

6 oz **raw jumbo shrimp**,
peeled

4 **scallions**

6 **mint leaves**

2 tablespoons **grapefruit
juice**

½ tablespoon **Thai fish sauce**
(nam pla)

1 large **red chili**, seeded and
finely sliced

pinch of **dried red pepper
flakes** or **black pepper**

pinch of **grated nutmeg**

4-5 **frisée** (curly-leaved
chicory) or **lollo rosso**
leaves

Cut the pomelo in half and scoop out the segments and juice. Discard the pith and thick skin surrounding each segment and break the flesh into small pieces. Stir the peanuts into the pomelo flesh. Set aside to allow the flavors to blend.

Bring a saucepan of water to a boil and simmer the shrimp for 1-2 minutes or until they turn pink and are cooked through. Remove them with a slotted spoon and drain well.

Finely shred the scallions and mint leaves. Add the shrimp to the pomelo flesh with the grapefruit juice, fish sauce, scallions, and mint.

Sprinkle the red chili, pepper, or pepper flakes, and nutmeg over the salad and toss together. Line the inside of a bowl with salad leaves and spoon in the shrimp and pomelo mixture. Serve immediately.

For pomelo & shrimp salad with vermicelli noodles,

put 5 oz vermicelli noodles into a large bowl and cover with boiling hot water. Allow to stand for 5 minutes or until the noodles are cooked through. Beat the juice of 1 lime, 1 tablespoon sweet chili sauce, and 1 teaspoon fish sauce. Drain the noodles and pour the dressing over them. Toss well to combine. Prepare the rest of the salad as above, but omitting the salad leaves. Toss all the ingredients together, garnish with peanuts and roughly chopped herbs, and serve immediately.

spicy lamb & couscous salad

Serves **4**

Preparation time **30 minutes**,
  plus marinating

Cooking time **15 minutes**

13 oz **lamb**

2 teaspoons **ras el hanout**

3 tablespoons **vegetable oil**

1 cup **couscous**

¾ cup hot **chicken stock**

small bunch of **cilantro**

2 **preserved lemons**

⅓ cup ready-to-eat **dried
  apricots**, chopped

3 tablespoons **currants**

salt and **pepper**

Dressing

4 tablespoons **yogurt**

¼ teaspoon **ras el hanout**

1 tablespoon chopped
  cilantro

2 tablespoons **lemon juice**

Cut the lamb into 1 inch dice. Beat together the ras el hanout and vegetable oil and marinate the lamb for at least 1 hour or overnight if possible.

Thread the meat onto metal or presoaked wooden skewers, putting about 6 pieces of lamb on each one.

Meanwhile, put the couscous in a bowl, add the hot chicken stock, cover, and allow to stand. Chop the cilantro, reserving some leaves for garnish. Remove and finely chop the peel from the preserved lemons and chop the apricots. Add the preserved lemon to the cooked couscous with the cilantro, apricots, and currants, season with salt and pepper and mix lightly.

Make the dressing by mixing all the ingredients in a small bowl. Set aside.

Cook the lamb skewers on a preheated hot griddle pan for 3–4 minutes each side until cooked through. Spoon the couscous onto serving plates and top each with 2–3 skewers and some yogurt dressing.

For vegetarian couscous salad, prepare the couscous as above, but using ¾ cup hot vegetable stock. Halve 5 Thai eggplants lengthwise, drizzle with olive oil, and cook on a hot griddle. Set aside. Cut 2 zucchini into long ribbons and 1 small sweet potato into strips and griddle. Put all the vegetables in a baking pan, drizzle with olive oil, salt, and pepper and cook in a preheated oven, 375°F, for 15 minutes until tender. Serve the vegetables on the couscous with the yogurt dressing.

celery, artichoke, & chicken salad

Serves **4–6**
Preparation time **15 minutes**
Cooking time **5 minutes**

6 thin slices of **rye bread**
2 tablespoons **olive oil**
1 leafy **celery head**
3½ oz canned or bottled
  artichoke hearts, drained
  and broiled
2 tablespoons roughly
  chopped **parsley**
3 smoked **chicken breasts**,
  each about 4 oz
salt and **pepper**

Dressing
1 teaspoon **Dijon mustard**
2 tablespoons **white wine**
  vinegar
4 tablespoons **olive oil**

Arrange the rye bread slices on a baking sheet. Drizzle with olive oil, season with salt and pepper, and bake in a preheated oven, 375°F, for 5 minutes until crispy like croutons. Remove from the oven and set aside.

Remove the leaves from the celery, reserving all the inside leaves. Finely slice 3 sticks and put them in a large salad bowl with the leaves, add the artichokes and parsley.

Thinly slice the smoked chicken breasts and add to the bowl with the celery and artichokes.

Make the dressing by beating together the mustard, vinegar, and oil. Drizzle over the salad and lightly mix.

Place a piece of rye toast on each serving plate and top with some salad.

For smoked chicken & cannellini bean salad, rinse and drain a 13½ oz can of cannellini beans and put them in a large salad bowl. Add 3 oz sun-blushed tomatoes, 4 oz blanched green beans, 3½ oz broiled artichokes and 3 roughly chopped smoked chicken breasts, each about 4 oz. In a small bowl beat 1 tablespoon chopped parsley, 1 tablespoon chopped basil, 1 teaspoon chopped tarragon, 1 crushed garlic clove, 2 tablespoons chardonnay vinegar, and 4 tablespoons olive oil. Season with salt and pepper. Toss the dressing through the salad and serve.

beef & cucumber salad

Serves **4**

Preparation time **15 minutes**, plus standing

Cooking time **12 minutes**

2 trimmed lean **porterhouse** or **sirloin** steaks, each about 5 oz

5 oz **baby corn ears**

1 large **cucumber**

1 small **red onion**, finely chopped

3 tablespoons chopped **cilantro leaves**

4 tablespoons **rice wine vinegar**

4 tablespoons **sweet chili dipping sauce**

2 tablespoons **sesame seeds**, to garnish

Put the steaks on a preheated hot griddle pan and cook for 3–4 minutes on each side. Allow to rest for 10–15 minutes then slice thinly.

Put the corn in a saucepan of boiling water and cook for 3–4 minutes or until tender. Refresh under cold water and drain well.

Slice the cucumber in half lengthwise, then scoop out and discard the seeds using a small spoon. Cut the cucumber into ¼ inch slices.

Put the onion in a large salad bowl with the beef, corn, cucumber, and chopped cilantro. Stir in the rice wine vinegar and chili sauce and mix well. Garnish the salad with lightly toasted sesame seeds and serve.

For beef salad with roasted shallots, peel about 20 shallots and put them on a baking sheet. Drizzle with olive oil and season with salt and pepper. Roast in a preheated oven, 375°F, for 20 minutes until golden and soft. In a small bowl mix 1 teaspoon Dijon mustard, 2 tablespoons cabernet sauvignon vinegar, 1 tablespoon chopped thyme, and 4 tablespoons olive oil. Cook the steaks as above and allow to rest, then finely slice and mix the meat with the roast shallots and 3 cups watercress. Drizzle over the dressing and serve immediately.

pomelo, shrimp, & pork salad

Serves **4**
Preparation time **20 minutes**
Cooking time **10–15 minutes**

8 oz **belly pork**
2 **pomelos**, peeled and
    segmented
7 oz **peeled, cooked jumbo
    shrimp**
small bunch of **mint**,
    separated into leaves
small bunch of **cilantro**,
    roughly chopped
small bunch of **Thai basil**,
    roughly chopped
3 tablespoons roughly
    chopped **roasted peanuts**,
    to garnish

Dressing
6 tablespoons **palm sugar**
juice of 2 **limes**
2 tablespoons **Thai fish
    sauce** (nam pla)
2 tablespoons **water**

Cut the belly pork into pieces about ¾–¼ inch. Heat
a skillet over a high heat and cook the pork for
4 minutes until golden and crispy, then drain on
paper towels.

Make the dressing. Put the sugar in a small, heavy
saucepan and cook for 4 minutes over a medium heat
until the sugar is bubbling and has turned a deep
caramel color. Carefully, because it might spit, beat in
the lime juice, fish sauce, and water. Remove from the
heat and set aside to cool slightly.

Combine the pomelo segments, the shrimp, the herbs,
and the cooked pork belly in a large salad bowl. Toss
lightly and transfer the salad to serving plates. Drizzle
the caramel dressing over the top, garnish with roasted
peanuts, and serve.

For pomelo, shrimp, pork, & shallot salad, add
fried shallots to the above. You can buy these ready-
prepared in Asian markets or make your own. Heat
2 cups vegetable oil in a heavy skillet or wok. Heat
the oil to 325°F and add 3 finely sliced shallots,
stirring constantly to make sure they cook evenly.
When they are golden, carefully remove them from
the oil with a slotted spoon and drain on paper
towels. Add to the salad above with the pomelo,
shrimp, pork, and herbs.

warm
salads

roast tomato & asparagus salad

Serves **4**
Preparation time **20 minutes**
Cooking time **2 hours**

2 large **beefsteak tomatoes**
6 tablespoons **olive oil**
2 **garlic cloves**
4 sprigs of **thyme**
bunch of **wild garlic**, roughly
  chopped
½ bunch of **basil**, roughly
  chopped
1 tablespoon **white wine
  vinegar**
24 **asparagus spears**,
  trimmed
grated **Parmesan cheese**
½ cup **arugula**
salt and **pepper**

Halve each tomato horizontally and put them, cut side up, on a baking sheet. Drizzle ½ teaspoon olive oil over each, season with salt and pepper, half a crushed garlic clove, and a sprig of thyme. Cook in a preheated oven, 225°F, for at least 2 hours. The tomatoes should be slightly dehydrated but still juicy.

Whiz the wild garlic, basil, and 5 tablespoons olive oil in a food processor. The garlic should still be slightly chunky. Place in a bowl and beat in the vinegar. Season with salt and pepper.

Arrange the asparagus on a dish and drizzle over ½ tablespoon oil. Season with a little salt and pepper. Heat a griddle pan over a high heat and cook the asparagus for about 5 minutes, turning the spears every 1–2 minutes. They will be just tender in the middle. Return the asparagus to the dish, cover with plastic wrap, and allow to steam slightly.

Remove the tomatoes from the oven and arrange on serving plates. Top each tomato with 6 asparagus spears, a drizzle of the wild garlic dressing, and a sprinkling of Parmesan cheese. Add the arugula beside the tomato and serve at once.

For tomato & mozzarella pasta salad, cook 8 oz penne until just tender, refresh in cold water, drizzle with olive oil, and reserve. Chop 2 beefsteak tomatoes into chunks and stir through the pasta. Drizzle over olive oil and 2 tablespoons balsamic vinegar and salt and pepper. Mix through ½ bunch torn basil leaves and 2 mozzarella balls, each about 5 oz, torn into 2–3 pieces, and serve.

chickpea & pepper salad

Serves **4**

Preparation time **25 minutes**

Cooking time **35 minutes**

2 x 13½ oz cans **chickpeas**

2 **red bell peppers**, cored, seeded, and halved

1 **yellow bell pepper**, cored, seeded, and halved

1 **red onion**, quartered but held together by the root

4 **plum tomatoes**, cut into wedges

olive oil

2 tablespoons **fennel seeds**

small bunch of **parsley**, chopped

salt and **pepper**

tzatziki (see below), to serve

Dressing

4 tablespoons **sherry vinegar**

3 tablespoons **olive oil**

1 **garlic clove**, crushed

½ teaspoon **ground cumin**

Rinse the chickpeas in cold water and allow to drain.

Drizzle the peppers, onions, and tomatoes with olive oil and salt and pepper. Heat a griddle pan over a high heat and cook the peppers for 2 minutes on each side. Slice the peppers into ¾ inch strips and place in an ovenproof dish then cook the onion in the same way. Place the onion and tomatoes with the peppers, sprinkle with fennel seeds, and cook in a preheated oven, 350°F, for 20 minutes until done.

Meanwhile, make the dressing. Beat together the vinegar and oil with the crushed garlic and cumin.

Transfer the drained chickpeas to a large salad bowl and mix in the hot vegetables and chopped parsley. Season to taste with salt and pepper, drizzle over the dressing and stir to combine. Serve with a dollop of tzatziki, if desired.

For tzatziki, to serve with the above salad, cut a cucumber in half lengthwise and remove the seeds with a spoon. Finely dice the flesh and mix it with 1 cup Greek or whole milk yogurt, 1 crushed garlic clove, 1 tablespoon olive oil, 2 tablespoons chopped mint, and 1 tablespoon lemon juice. Season to taste with salt and pepper, cover, and leave in the refrigerator for at least 1 hour before serving.

scallop, parsnip, & carrot salad

Serves **4**
Preparation time **15 minutes**
Cooking time **30 minutes**

4 **carrots**, quartered
   lengthwise
3 **parsnips**, quartered
   lengthwise
2 tablespoons **olive oil**
1 tablespoon **cumin seeds**
12 fresh **sea scallops**
2 tablespoons **lemon juice**
salt and **pepper**
chopped **parsley**, to garnish

Dressing
4 tablespoons **plain yogurt**
2 tablespoons **lemon juice**
2 tablespoons **olive oil**
1 teaspoon **ground cumin**

Put the carrots and parsnips on a foil-lined baking sheet. Drizzle with 1 tablespoon of the oil, sprinkle with the cumin seeds, season with salt and pepper, and cook in a preheated oven, 350°F, for 20–25 minutes.

Meanwhile, make the dressing. Mix the yogurt, lemon juice, oil, and ground cumin in a small bowl. Season to taste with salt and pepper.

Trim the scallops to remove the tough muscle on the outside of the white fleshy part. Heat the remaining oil in a large skillet and fry the scallops for 2 minutes on each side until they are just cooked through. Pour over the lemon juice and transfer the scallops and cooking juices to a large salad bowl.

Add the carrots and parsnips to the bowl and mix, then transfer them to a serving dish, spoon over the yogurt dressing, garnish with parsley, and serve.

For curried scallops & carrot salad, roast 4 carrots and 3 parsnips as above but omit the cumin. Combine 1 tablespoon curry powder with 2 cups milk and 4 tablespoons butter. Soften 2 tablespoons cornstarch with a little of the milk and beat to combine. Transfer the mixture to a small, heavy saucepan and bring to a boil, beating all the time so that lumps do not form. When you have a smooth, thickened sauce drop in the scallops and cook them for 3 minutes. Transfer the carrots and parsnips to a serving plate, arrange the scallops on top, and serve with the sauce.

asian salmon salad

Serves **4**
Preparation time **20 minutes**
Cooking time **8–10 minutes**

¾ cup **long-grain rice**
4 **salmon fillets**, each about
    4 oz
3 tablespoons **tamari sauce**
4 oz **sugar snap peas**, halved
    lengthwise
1 large **carrot**, cut into
    matchsticks
4 **scallions**, thinly sliced
1½ cups **bean sprouts**
6 teaspoons **sunflower oil**
3 tablespoons **sesame seeds**
2 teaspoons **Thai fish sauce**
    (nam pla) (optional)
2 teaspoons **rice vinegar** or
    white wine vinegar
small bunch of **cilantro** or
    basil, leaves roughly torn

Half-fill a saucepan with water and bring to a boil. Add the rice and simmer for 8 minutes.

Meanwhile, put the salmon on a foil-lined broiler rack and drizzle over 1 tablespoon of the tamari sauce. Cook under a preheated broiler for 8–10 minutes, turning once, until the fish is browned and flakes easily.

Add the sugar snap peas to the rice and cook for 1 minute. Drain, rinse with cold water, and drain again. Tip into a salad bowl. Add the carrot, scallions, and bean sprouts to the salad bowl.

Heat 1 teaspoon of the oil in a nonstick skillet, add the sesame seeds and fry until just beginning to brown. Add 1 tablespoon tamari sauce and quickly cover the pan so that the seeds do not ping out. Remove the pan from the heat and let stand for 1–2 minutes, then mix in the remaining tamari sauce, oil, fish sauce (if used), and vinegar.

Add the sesame mixture to the salad and toss together. Take the skin off the salmon and flake into pieces, discarding any bones. Add to the salad with the torn herb leaves and serve immediately.

For Asian tofu salad, cut 8 oz firm tofu into ¼ inch slices. Mix 2 tablespoons soy sauce, 1 tablespoon sweet chili sauce, and 1 teaspoon sesame oil and marinate the tofu for at least 1 hour. Prepare the salad as above but omit the salmon. When the salad is ready, heat a nonstick skillet and fry the tofu for 2–3 minutes on each side. Serve on top of the salad with any remaining marinade.

chorizo, pepper, & oregano salad

Serves **2–4**
Preparation time **15 minutes**
Cooking time **15 minutes**

1 **red onion**
2 **red bell peppers**
2 **yellow bell peppers**
7 oz **chorizo sausage**
1 tablespoon **olive oil**
2 tablespoons **sherry vinegar**
½ bunch of **oregano**, roughly
   chopped
1½ cups **arugula**
salt and **pepper**
romesco sauce (see below),
   to serve

Finely dice the red onion. Core and seed the peppers and cut the flesh into ¾ inch squares. Slice the chorizo.

Heat the oil in a large skillet over a high heat and cook the peppers for 2–3 minutes until they start to brown. Add the chorizo and fry for another 3 minutes, then reduce the heat to low and add the onion. Cook for an additional 3 minutes. Deglaze the pan with the sherry vinegar and reduce for 1 minute.

Transfer the contents of the pan to a large salad bowl and allow to cool slightly, then toss with the oregano and arugula. Season with salt and pepper and serve with romesco sauce.

For romesco sauce, to serve with the above salad, soak 1 dried anchero chili in water for 1 hour, then drain. Put 4 ready-marinated red sweet peppers, the anchero chili, 2 peeled and seeded tomatoes, 2 tablespoons blanched toasted almonds and 3 tablespoons roasted hazelnuts, 1 garlic clove, 1 tablespoon red wine vinegar, and 1 teaspoon smoked paprika into a food processor or blender and whiz briefly to make a smooth sauce. Season to taste with salt and pepper and serve with the salad.

chicken couscous salad

Serves **4**

Preparation time **20 minutes**, plus marinating

Cooking time **20 minutes**

4 boneless, skinless **chicken breasts**, each about 4 oz

1½ cups **couscous**

1¼ cups hot **chicken stock**

1 **pomegranate**

zest and **juice** of 1 **orange**

small bunch of **cilantro**

small bunch of **mint**

Marinade

1½ tablespoons **curry paste (tikka masala)**

5 tablespoons **plain yogurt**

1 teaspoon **olive oil**

2 tablespoons **lemon juice**

Make a marinade by mixing the curry paste, yogurt, and oil. Put the chicken in a nonmetallic dish, cover with half the marinade, and leave for at least 1 hour.

Put the couscous in a bowl, add the hot stock, cover, and leave for 8 minutes.

Meanwhile, cut the pomegranate in half and remove the seeds. Add them to the couscous with the orange zest and juice.

Remove the chicken from the marinade, reserving the marinade, and transfer to a foil-lined baking sheet. Cook in a preheated oven, 375°F, for 6–7 minutes, then transfer to a preheated hot broiler and cook for 2 minutes until caramelized. Cover with foil and allow to rest for 5 minutes.

Roughly chop the cilantro and mint, reserving some whole cilantro leaves for garnish, and add to the couscous. Thinly slice the chicken. Spoon the couscous onto plates and add the chicken. Thin the reserved marinade with the lemon juice and drizzle over the couscous. Garnish with the reserved cilantro leaves and serve immediately.

For pomegranate vinaigrette, an alternative dressing for this salad, beat together ⅔ cup pomegranate juice, 2 tablespoons pomegranate molasses (available from Middle Eastern markets and some supermarkets), 2 tablespoons red wine vinegar, and 3 tablespoons olive oil.

pumpkin, feta, & pine nut salad

Serves **4**
Preparation time **20 minutes**
Cooking time
about **25 minutes**

1 lb **pumpkin**
olive oil
2 sprigs of **thyme**, roughly
chopped
4 cups **mixed baby salad
leaves**
2 oz **feta cheese**
salt and **pepper**
2 tablespoons **toasted pine
nuts**, to garnish

Dressing
1 teaspoon **Dijon mustard**
2 tablespoons **balsamic
vinegar**
4 tablespoons **olive oil**

Skin and seed the pumpkin, cut the flesh into ¾ inch squares and put them in a roasting pan. Drizzle with olive oil, sprinkle with the thyme, and season with salt and pepper. Roast the pumpkin in a preheated oven, 375°F, for 25 minutes or until cooked though. Remove the pumpkin from the oven and allow to cool slightly.

Meanwhile, make the dressing. Beat together the mustard, vinegar, and oil and set aside.

Put the mixed leaves in a large salad bowl, add the cooked pumpkin, and crumble in the feta. Drizzle over the dressing and toss carefully to combine. Transfer the mixture to serving plates, garnish with toasted pine nuts, and serve immediately.

For roast pumpkin, bacon, sage, & pasta salad, prepare the pumpkin as above, but using 2 sprigs of sage instead of thyme. Cook 8 oz penne until it is just tender, drain, and refresh in cold water. Finely slice 8 oz bacon and fry until golden, add 10 sage leaves to the pan and fry until crispy. Remove from the pan and drain on paper towels. Combine all the ingredients in a large salad bowl, add 2 cups mixed baby salad leaves, 2 oz feta cheese and season with salt and pepper. Drizzle over olive oil and serve.

balsamic roast vegetable salad

Serves **4**

Preparation time **20 minutes**

Cooking time **30 minutes**

1 **red onion**, roughly chopped

4 **carrots**, roughly chopped

1 **red bell pepper**, cored, seeded and cut into large pieces

1 **sweet potato**, peeled and cut into even-sized pieces

13 oz **zucchini**, peeled and cut into even-sized pieces

1 **butternut squash**, about 2 lb, peeled, seeded, and cut into chunks

2 tablespoons **olive oil**, plus extra to drizzle

⅔ cup **balsamic vinegar**

1 tablespoon chopped **thyme**

1 tablespoon chopped **rosemary**

1½ cups **arugula**

salt and **pepper**

Put all the vegetables in a roasting pan and coat well with the oil and balsamic vinegar and add the herbs. Season to taste with salt and pepper and roast in a preheated oven, 375°F, for 30 minutes until they are cooked and slightly crispy.

Remove the vegetables from the oven, allow to cool slightly, then toss with the arugula. Drizzle with olive oil, check the seasoning, and serve.

For herb-crusted rack of lamb with vegetable salad, put ½ cup butter, 2 cups bread crumbs, 2 tablespoons chopped thyme, 2 tablespoons chopped rosemary, 2 cups chopped parsley, 2 crushed garlic cloves, and ½ cup grated Parmesan cheese into a food processor or blender. Season to taste with salt and pepper and whiz to make a smooth paste. Remove the spiced butter from the food processor, place it between 2 pieces of waxed paper and roll it out to ¼ inch thick. Put the butter in the refrigerator to chill. Heat 1 tablespoon vegetable oil in a large skillet over a high heat and seal 2 x 4-point racks of lamb until golden. Cook the lamb in a preheated oven, 375°C, for about 12 minutes or until just cooked through. Remove the lamb from the oven and cut a piece of butter to fit over each rack. Cook both racks under a preheated hot broiler until golden. Let rest for 5 minutes, then slice and serve with the vegetable salad as above.

smoked salmon & potato salad

Serves **4**

Preparation time **15 minutes**

Cooking time **20 minutes**

1¼ lb **new potatoes**

2 tablespoons small **capers**

3 tablespoons **Mayonnaise**
(see page 12)

2 tablespoons **lemon juice**

1 teaspoon grated
horseradish

5 oz **smoked salmon**

punnet of **mustard** and **cress**,
trimmed

salt and **pepper**

Put the potatoes in a saucepan of lightly salted cold water, bring to a boil, and cook for 15–20 minutes or until just cooked through. Drain the potatoes and let them cool slightly.

Meanwhile, chop the capers and combine them with the mayonnaise, lemon juice, and horseradish. Season to taste with salt and pepper. Put the warm potatoes in a large salad bowl, add the mayonnaise dressing, and stir to combine thoroughly.

Arrange the salmon on 4 plates, top with the potatoes, and garnish with mustard and cress.

For roast beef & wholegrain mustard potato salad, seal a 1 lb piece of beef tenderloin until golden, then cook in a preheated oven, 350°F, for 15 minutes until cooked to medium rare. Remove, cover with foil, and allow to rest. Mix 3 tablespoons mayonnaise, 2 tablespoons wholegrain mustard, 1 teaspoon Dijon mustard, and 5 finely sliced scallions. Mix through 1¼ lb cooked new potatoes and combine well. Thinly slice the beef and serve with the mustard potato salad.

asparagus & arugula salad

Serves **4**
Preparation time **15 minutes**
Cooking time about **5 minutes**

3 tablespoons **olive oil**
   (optional)
1 lb **asparagus**
½ cup **Tarragon & Lemon**
   Dressing (see page 14)
2½ cups **arugula** or other
   salad leaves
2 **scallions**, finely sliced
4 **radishes**, finely sliced
salt and **pepper**

To garnish
herbs, such as **tarragon,**
   parsley, chervil, and **dill,**
   roughly chopped
thin strips of **lemon rind**

Heat the oil (if used) in a large, nonstick skillet and add the asparagus in a single layer. Cook for about 5 minutes, turning occasionally. The asparagus should be tender when pierced with the tip of a sharp knife and lightly patched with brown. Remove from the pan to a shallow dish and sprinkle with salt and pepper. Cover with the tarragon and lemon dressing, toss gently, and let stand for 5 minutes.

Arrange the arugula on a serving plate. Sprinkle the scallions and radishes over the arugula. Arrange the asparagus in a pile in the center of the arugula. Garnish with herbs and lemon rind. Serve the salad on its own with bread or as an accompaniment to a main dish.

For broiled asparagus with bacon, remove the woody ends from a large bunch of asparagus, about 1 lb. Individually wrap the asparagus spears in pieces of bacon, making sure that the bacon covers the base of each spear. Arrange the asparagus in a single layer on a baking sheet and place under a preheated hot broiler for 5–7 minutes, turning occasionally until golden and cooked through. Serve the asparagus with the arugula salad as above and drizzle over the tarragon and lemon dressing.

grilled vegetable & haloumi salad

Serves **4**
Preparation time **15 minutes**
Cooking time **25 minutes**

12 **cherry tomatoes on the vine**
4 **portobello mushrooms**
olive oil
2 **zucchini**
1 lb **asparagus**
8 oz **haloumi cheese**
salt and **pepper**

Dressing
2 tablespoons **olive oil**
2 tablespoons **balsamic vinegar**

Put the tomatoes and mushrooms in a roasting pan, drizzle with about 2 tablespoons oil, season to taste with salt and pepper, and cook in a preheated oven, 350°F, for 10 minutes.

Meanwhile, cut the zucchini into batons about 1½ x ¾ inch and put them in a large bowl with the trimmed asparagus. Drizzle with olive oil and a pinch of salt and pepper. Heat a griddle pan over a high heat and grill the asparagus and zucchini. Transfer the asparagus and zucchini to the oven with the other vegetables and cook for an additional 6–8 minutes.

Cut the haloumi into ¼ inch slices. Heat 1 teaspoon olive oil in a large skillet over a medium heat and cook the cheese slices until golden.

Make the dressing by beating the oil and vinegar. Stack the vegetables on serving plates, top with slices of cheese, spoon over the dressing, and serve.

For watermelon & haloumi cheese, cut 8 oz haloumi into thin slices. Heat 1 tablespoon olive oil in a large, nonstick skillet and cook the cheese until golden and crispy. Drain and pat dry with paper towels. Peel and seed half a small watermelon and cut it into small triangles. Toss the melon with a small bunch of chopped mint and the diced flesh of 1 ripe avocado. Serve with the grilled haloumi.

roast mushroom salad

Serves **2**
Preparation time **10 minutes**
Cooking time **20 minutes**

2 **portobello mushrooms**,
   each about 5 oz
3 tablespoons **olive oil**
1 tablespoon **balsamic
   vinegar**
1 cup large **bread crumbs**
3 sprigs of **thyme**, chopped
½ cup **mixed arugula,
   watercress, and spinach
   leaves**
salt and **pepper**

Dressing
4 oz **soft goat cheese**
2 tablespoons **olive oil**
2 tablespoons **milk**

Put the mushrooms in a roasting pan and drizzle over 1 tablespoon of the olive oil and the balsamic vinegar. Cook in a preheated oven, 350°F, for 20 minutes.

Meanwhile, spread the bread crumbs on a baking sheet with the thyme leaves. Pour over the remaining oil and season with salt and pepper. Place in the oven and cook for 6–8 minutes until golden and crispy.

Make the dressing. Put the cheese, oil, and milk in a small saucepan and beat over a gentle heat until the mixture reaches a pouring consistency, adding a little more milk if it is too thick.

Transfer the mushrooms to serving plates and top with the bread crumbs. Arrange a handful of the mixed leaves to the side and drizzle with the warm dressing. Serve immediately.

For roast mushroom & prosciutto salad, place 4 slices of prosciutto on a baking sheet and cook in a preheated oven, 350°F, for 4–5 minutes until crispy. Prepare the mushrooms and bread crumbs as above and serve the crispy prosciutto with the mushrooms and salad leaves.

squid, fennel, & potato salad

Serves **4**

Preparation time **15 minutes,
plus cooling**

Cooking time **30 minutes**

8 oz **new potatoes**
2 **fennel bulbs**
3 tablespoons **olive oil**
1 lb prepared **squid**
2 cups **watercress**, separated
into leaves
salt and **pepper**

Dressing
1 **shallot**, finely chopped
1 red **chili**, seeded and
chopped
zest and **juice** of 1 **lemon**
1 tablespoon chopped **capers**
1 tablespoon chopped **mint**
2 tablespoons **olive oil**

Put the potatoes in a saucepan of lightly salted cold water, bring to a boil, and cook for 15–20 minutes or until just cooked through. Drain the potatoes and allow them to cool.

Reserving the fronds for garnish, cut the fennel into thin wedges, leaving the root end intact to hold the pieces together. Put the fennel in a baking pan, drizzle with 1 tablespoon of the oil, season with salt and pepper, and cook in a preheated oven, 375°F, for 15 minutes until roasted and golden.

Meanwhile, cut the potatoes in half. Heat 1 tablespoon of the oil in a skillet and fry the potatoes until they are crisp and golden. Drain on paper towels and transfer to a large salad bowl.

Make the dressing. Mix all the ingredients in a bowl.

Heat the remaining oil in a large skillet until it is smoking and carefully fry the squid for 2–3 minutes. Add the squid to the bowl. Remove the fennel from the oven, let cool slightly and add to the bowl with the dressing and combine gently. Stir through the watercress and serve at once.

For chili squid salad, mix together 5 tablespoons all-purpose flour, 1 tablespoon chili powder and 1 teaspoon salt. Dust 1 lb prepared squid pieces in the seasoned flour and deep-fry in hot oil for 2 minutes until golden and crunchy. Serve with sliced chili, fresh cilantro and mint leaves, sliced scallions, and lime wedges.

warm tea-smoked salmon salad

Serves **4**
Preparation time **15 minutes**,
  plus resting
Cooking time **10 minutes**

4 **salmon fillets**, each about
  4 oz
4 oz **cherry tomatoes**, halved
2½ cups **arugula**

Smoke mix
8 tablespoons **jasmine tea
  leaves**
8 tablespoons **brown sugar**
8 tablespoons **long-grain rice**

Dressing
1 **shallot**, finely chopped
1 **garlic clove**, finely chopped
thyme leaves
1 teaspoon **Dijon mustard**
2 teaspoons **white wine
  vinegar**
4–5 tablespoons **olive oil**
salt and **pepper**

Mix together all the ingredients for the smoke mix. Line a wok with a large sheet of foil, allowing it to overhang the edges, and pour in the smoke mix. Place a trivet over the top. Cover with a tight-fitting lid and heat for 5 minutes or until the mixture is smoking.

Meanwhile, remove any bones from the salmon with tweezers. Put the tomatoes and arugula in a bowl.

Quickly remove the lid from the wok and place the salmon fillets, skin side down, on the trivet. Cover and cook over a high heat for 5 minutes. Remove from the heat and set aside, covered, for another 3 minutes.

Meanwhile, make the dressing. Mix the shallot and garlic in a bowl with the thyme leaves, mustard, vinegar, oil, and salt and pepper. Beat thoroughly to combine.

Flake the salmon into the tomato and arugula salad, add the dressing, and toss well. Serve immediately.

For tea-smoked salmon with buckwheat noodle salad, prepare the salmon as above and set aside. Boil 5 oz buckwheat noodles for 3 minutes or until just tender. Strain and refresh in cold water, then stir in 1 tablespoon sesame oil and the zest and juice of 1 lime. Add a little more oil if the noodles are sticking together. Mix ½ cup white vinegar, 2 tablespoons water, and 3 tablespoons superfine sugar and stir over a gentle heat until the sugar has dissolved. Allow to cool completely. Finely slice ½ cucumber, add to the cool liquid, and infuse for 1 hour. Remove the cucumber from the pickle, mix with the noodles and 2½ cups arugula and serve with the salmon.

chorizo & quails' egg salad

Serves **4**

Preparation time **15 minutes**

Cooking time **15–20 minutes**

3 tablespoons **olive oil**

7 oz medium-hot **chorizo sausage**

1 small **red onion**, cut into wedges

1 **garlic clove**, chopped

1 teaspoon **smoked paprika**

1 teaspoon **dried oregano**

8–12 **quails' eggs**

6 cups **baby spinach leaves**

1 tablespoon **aged sherry vinegar**

1 tablespoon **salted capers** or **capers in brine**

2 tablespoons chopped **chives**

Heat 1 tablespoon of the oil in a large skillet over a moderately high heat. Thickly slice the chorizo and fry for about 3 minutes until crisp and golden.

Add the onion and garlic to the skillet and continue cooking for 2 minutes until the onion is wilted and browned but not completely soft. Stir in the paprika and oregano and remove from the heat.

Bring a small pan of water to a gentle simmering point. Crack a quail's egg into a small saucer, then drop it carefully into the simmering water. Leave for 1 minute, then remove with a slotted spoon and place on paper towels. Keep the egg warm while you poach the remaining eggs.

Wash and dry the spinach leaves and stir them quickly into the chorizo mixture with the remaining olive oil and the sherry vinegar. Arrange on serving plates, sprinkle with rinsed and drained capers, and top each one with 2–3 quails' eggs. Sprinkle the eggs with the chives and serve immediately.

For spinach, chorizo, & lentil salad, cook 1 cup Puy lentils according to the instructions on the package, flavoring the water with 1 red chili sliced lengthwise, 2 crushed garlic cloves, and 1 teaspoon cumin. Drain the lentils and keep them warm. Prepare the salad as above, mix the lentils through the other ingredients, dress with 1 tablespoon each sherry vinegar and olive oil, and serve topped with poached quail eggs.

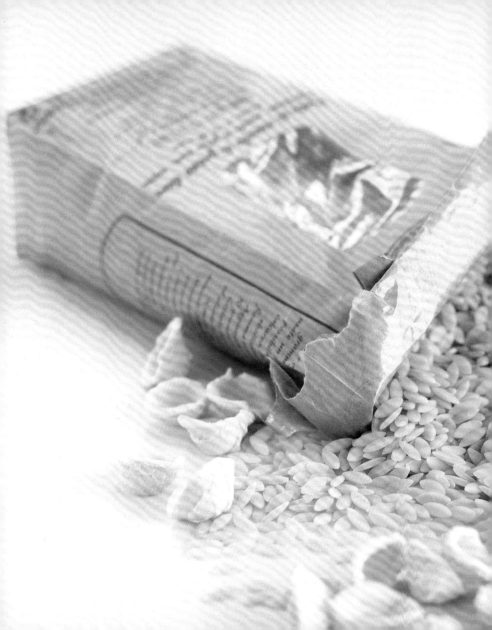

rice, beans,
grains, &
pasta

sushi rice salad

Serves **2–3**
Preparation time **20 minutes,
plus cooling**
Cooking time **30 minutes**

1¼ cups **sushi rice**
6 tablespoons **rice wine
vinegar**
2½ tablespoons **superfine
sugar**
small piece of **pickled ginger,**
chopped
½ teaspoon **wasabi**
½ **cucumber**
1 **avocado**, about 6 oz, peeled
and cut into small cubes
8 oz **skinless salmon**, cut into
bite-size pieces
8 **scallions**, finely sliced

To garnish
3 tablespoons **toasted
sesame seeds**

Cook the rice according to instructions on the package.

Meanwhile, put the vinegar and sugar in a small saucepan and heat gently, stirring, until the sugar has dissolved. Turn off the heat and add the chopped pickled ginger and wasabi. Allow to cool. Cut the cucumber in half lengthwise and scoop out the seeds with a teaspoon. Slice the flesh finely and add to the cooled vinegar mix.

When the rice is cooked transfer it to a dish, strain the vinegar mixture over it, reserving the cucumber, stir and let cool.

Transfer the cooled rice to a large salad bowl and combine gently with the cucumber, salmon, avocado, and scallions. Top with the toasted sesame seeds and serve.

For seared tuna & rice salad, mix 2 tablespoons soy sauce with ¼ teaspoon wasabi and brush 10 oz tuna loin with the mixture. Roll the tuna in sesame seeds until coated all over. Heat 1 tablespoon vegetable oil in a large skillet over a high heat and fry the tuna for 1–2 minutes on each side. Remove the tuna from the heat and allow to rest. Prepare the salad as above but omit the salmon. Thinly slice the tuna and serve with the sushi rice salad.

warm orzo salad

Serves **4**

Preparation time **15 minutes, plus resting**

Cooking time **12 minutes**

8 oz **orzo** or **malloreddus pasta**

1⅔ cups frozen **peas**, thawed

6 tablespoons **olive oil**

6 **scallions**, roughly chopped

2 **garlic cloves**, crushed

8 **marinated artichoke hearts**, thinly sliced

4 tablespoons chopped **mint**

zest and **juice** of ½ **lemon**

salt and **pepper**

grated **lemon zest**, to garnish

Cook the pasta in a saucepan of lightly salted boiling water for about 6 minutes or according to the instructions on the package. Add the thawed peas and cook for an additional 2–3 minutes until the peas and pasta are cooked. Drain well.

Meanwhile, heat 2 tablespoons oil in a skillet and stir-fry the scallions and garlic for 1–2 minutes until softened.

Stir the scallions and garlic into the pasta with the artichokes, mint, and the remaining oil. Toss well, season with salt and pepper, then let rest for 10 minutes. Stir in the lemon juice and serve the salad warm, garnished with lemon zest.

For warm pasta salad with lemony chicken, either ask your butcher to butterfly a chicken, about 2½ lb, for you or do it yourself by cutting down the backbone without cutting through the breast and pressing down on the chicken to flatten it. Mix 3 tablespoons olive oil, 2 tablespoons chopped mint, 2 tablespoons chopped parsley, the zest and juice of 1 lemon, and salt and pepper. Rub the mixture over the chicken and allow to marinate for at least 1 hour. Place the chicken, skin side up, in a foil-lined baking pan and cook in a preheated oven, 350°F, for about 40 minutes until cooked though. Allow the chicken to rest for 5 minutes, then cut it into bite-size pieces, arrange them on top of the pasta salad as above and serve with lemon wedges.

crab & orzo salad

Serves **4**
Preparation time **15 minutes**
Cooking time **20 minutes**

4 oz **orzo pasta**
13 oz white cooked **crabmeat**
7 oz **cherry tomatoes**
2½ cups **arugula**
zest and **juice** of 1 **lemon**
2 tablespoons chopped
   parsley
1 teaspoon small **capers**,
   rinsed
2 tablespoons **olive oil**

Chili mayonnaise
¾ cup **Mayonnaise**
   (see page 12)
1 marinated **red sweet
   pepper**
1 long **red chili**, roughly
   chopped
1 teaspoon **lemon juice**
salt and **pepper**

Cook the orzo in a large pan of boiling water according to the instructions on the package. Refresh and reserve.

Make the chili mayonnaise. Put the mayonnaise, red pepper, and red chili in a food processor or blender and whiz until smooth. Season to taste with salt and pepper and lemon juice.

Combine the crab and orzo in a large salad bowl. Halve the tomatoes and add them to the bowl with the arugula, lemon zest, parsley, and capers and mix carefully. Add 2 tablespoons lemon juice and the oil. Season with salt and pepper and serve with a dollop of the chili mayonnaise.

For herby mayonnaise, to serve as an alternative with the above salad, chop a mixture of herbs, including chives, chervil, dill, parsley, and mint, to make 4 tablespoons. Mix the chopped herbs with ¾ cup mayonnaise, the zest of 1 lemon, and 1 tablespoon lemon juice. Adjust the seasoning with salt and pepper and serve on top of the salad.

lentil & feta salad

Serves **2–4**
Preparation time **15 minutes**
Cooking time **30 minutes**

1¼ cups **Puy lentils**
2 **carrots**, finely diced
2 **celery sticks**, finely diced
4 oz **feta cheese**
2 tablespoons chopped
   parsley

Dressing
3 tablespoons **white wine
   vinegar**
2 teaspoons **Dijon mustard**
5 tablespoons **olive oil**
salt and **pepper**

Put the lentils in a saucepan, cover with cold water, and add a pinch of salt. Bring to a boil and cook for 20–25 minutes until just cooked but not mushy. Drain and refresh in cold water, then drain again and transfer to a large salad bowl.

Add the carrots and celery to the bowl with the lentils. Crumble in the feta and add the chopped parsley.

Make the dressing by beating the vinegar, mustard, and oil. Add the dressing to the salad and stir to combine well. Season to taste with salt and pepper and serve immediately.

For lentil salad with poached egg & asparagus, prepare the lentils as above. Blanch about 1 lb asparagus, woody ends removed, refresh and reserve. Cook 8 oz sliced pancetta under a preheated hot broiler until crispy. Slice the pancetta and asparagus into 1¼ inch pieces, add them to the lentils with 2 tablespoons chopped parsley and 5 tablespoons olive oil and season with salt and pepper. Toss carefully to combine and transfer to serving plates. Put a soft-poached egg on each salad and top with 1 tablespoon of hollandaise sauce on top of the egg.

curried couscous salad

Serves **4**
Preparation time **15 minutes**

juice of **1 orange**
2 teaspoons **mild curry paste**
1 cup **couscous**
⅓ cup **golden raisins**
1¼ cups boiling **water**
8 oz **smoked mackerel fillets**
1 small **red onion**, finely chopped
½ **red bell pepper**, cored, seeded, and diced
2 **tomatoes**, chopped
small bunch of **cilantro**, roughly chopped
pepper

Put the orange juice and curry paste into a bowl and stir together. Add the couscous, golden raisins, and a little pepper, then pour in the boiling water and fork together. Let stand for 5 minutes.

Meanwhile, peel the skin off the mackerel fillets and break the flesh into large flakes, discarding any bones.

Add the mackerel, onion, bell pepper, and tomatoes to the couscous and mix together lightly. Sprinkle roughly chopped cilantro over the top, spoon onto plates, and serve immediately.

For curried couscous salad with lamb chops, mix 4 tablespoons plain yogurt with 1 teaspoon mild curry paste. Marinate 12 lamb rib chops in the mixture. Prepare the couscous salad as above, omitting the mackerel. Heat 2 tablespoons vegetable oil in a large griddle pan over a high heat and grill the lamb for 3 minutes on each side until cooked through. Serve the lamb on the couscous salad, garnished with chopped cilantro.

bean, kabanos, & pepper salad

Serves **4**

Preparation time **10 minutes, plus cooling**

Cooking time **20 minutes**

3 **red bell peppers**, halved, cored, and seeded

1 **red chili**, seeded

1 tablespoon **olive oil**

1 **onion**, thinly sliced

3 oz **kabanos sausage**, thinly sliced

2 x 13 oz cans **lima beans** or **flageolet beans**, drained and rinsed

1 tablespoon **balsamic vinegar**

2 tablespoons chopped **cilantro**

Put the peppers and chili, skin side up, on a baking sheet under a hot broiler and cook for 10–12 minutes or until the skins are blackened. Transfer them to a plastic bag, fold over the top to seal and allow to cool. Peel off the skins and slice the flesh.

Meanwhile, heat the oil in a large, nonstick skillet, add the onion and fry for 5–6 minutes until soft. Add the sausage and fry for 1–2 minutes until crisp.

Put the beans in a large salad bowl. Add all the remaining ingredients and mix well. Serve the salad with walnut bread.

For beef kebabs with bean salad, mix together 1 teaspoon dried chili, 2 tablespoons sweet red pepper paste, 4 tablespoons olive oil, 1 finely sliced onion, 1 teaspoon ground cumin, and 1 teaspoon ground coriander. Marinate 13 oz diced beef in the mixture for at least 1 hour, then thread the meat onto metal or presoaked wooden skewers, alternating the meat with pieces of onion and green bell pepper. Cook under a preheated hot broiler for 4 minutes on each side until cooked through. Prepare the salad as above, omitting the kabanos sausage, and serve with the beef kebabs.

orecchiette, bacon, & broccoli salad

Serves **4**

Preparation time **15 minutes**

Cooking time **20 minutes**

8 oz **broccoli**

10 oz **orecchiette pasta**

5 oz **pancetta**

5 oz **cherry tomatoes**

Dressing

4 tablespoons **Mayonnaise** (see page 12)

2 tablespoons **light cream**

2½ tablespoons **tomato ketchup**

2 teaspoons **Worcestershire sauce**

3 drops **Tabasco sauce**

1 teaspoon **lemon juice**

salt and **pepper**

Separate the broccoli florets and slice the stems.

Meanwhile, bring a large saucepan of lightly salted water to a boil and cook the pasta for 10 minutes or according to the instructions on the package. Add the broccoli stems to the saucepan and cook for 2 minutes. Add the florets and cook for an additional minute. Drain and refresh in cold water. Transfer to a large salad bowl.

Cut the pancetta into matchsticks and dry-fry for 4 minutes until crispy and golden. Drain on paper towels and allow to cool before adding to the pasta. Halve the cherry tomatoes and add them to the pasta.

Make the dressing by combining all the ingredients. Season to taste with salt and pepper. Stir the dressing into the pasta and broccoli and serve immediately.

For warm broccoli & chicken salad, cook the pasta and broccoli as above but do not refresh in cold water. Shred 2 poached chicken breasts and stir the meat into the pasta with 5 oz halved cherry tomatoes, 3 tablespoons olive oil, 1 sliced red chili, and ½ cup grated Parmesan cheese. Garnish with extra grated Parmesan and 2 tablespoons each chopped parsley and chopped basil.

sardine & lentil salad

Serves **4**

Preparation time **15 minutes**

Cooking time **3 minutes**

⅔ cup frozen **peas**

2 x 3¾ oz cans boneless,
   skinless s**ardines in tomato
   sauce**

13½ oz can **green lentils**

2 inches **cucumber**

1 small **red onion**

small bunch of **mint**, roughly
   chopped

grated **zest** and **juice** of
   1 **lemon**

1 **romaine lettuce**

pepper

Cook the peas in a saucepan of boiling water for
3 minutes. Alternatively, cook them in the microwave
for 1½ minutes on full power.

Flake the sardines into chunks and put them in a large
salad bowl with their sauce. Rinse and drain the lentils,
dice the cucumber, and chop the onion. Add the lentils,
peas, cucumber, and onion to the sardines. Add the
mint to the salad with the lemon zest and juice and a
little pepper and toss together.

Separate the lettuce into leaves and arrange them
on serving plates. Spoon the sardine salad on top
and serve.

For potato, sardine, & lentil salad, crush 7 oz boiled
baby potatoes in their skins and put them in a baking
pan with 7 oz cherry tomatoes. Drizzle with olive oil,
salt and pepper, and 3 sprigs of thyme. Roast in a
preheated oven, 375°F, until golden and crispy, then
allow to cool till just warm. Meanwhile, mix together
3 tablespoons chopped parsley, 1 crushed garlic
clove, the zest and juice of 1 lemon, and 3 tablespoons
olive oil. Fry 4 fresh sardine fillets in a hot skillet for
2–3 minutes each side or until done. Mix the tomatoes
and potatoes with 1½ cups arugula, then serve with
the sardine fillets on top with the herb dressing
drizzled over.

buckwheat & salmon salad

Serves **4**
Preparation time **15 minutes**
Cooking time **20 minutes**

1½ cups **buckwheat**
8 oz **broccoli florets**
8 oz **cherry tomatoes,** halved
8 oz **smoked salmon**
small bunch of **parsley,**
  chopped
4 tablespoons chopped **dill**
salt and **pepper**

Dressing
juice of 1 **lemon**
3 tablespoons **olive oil**

Put the buckwheat in a saucepan, cover with cold water, and add a pinch of salt. Bring to a boil and cook for 10–15 minutes until still firm and not mushy. Drain under running cold water and remove the foam that accumulates. Drain again when cool.

Bring a large saucepan of lightly salted water to a boil and blanch the broccoli florets for 2–3 minutes. Refresh in cold water and drain.

Mix the cherry tomatoes with the buckwheat and broccoli in a large salad bowl. Slice the smoked salmon and add it to the bowl with the parsley and half of the dill.

Make the dressing by beating the lemon juice and oil. Pour the dressing over the salad, mix lightly to combine, and season to taste with salt and pepper. Garnish with the remaining dill and serve immediately.

For smoked salmon & spring green salad,
blanch and refresh 13 oz assorted green vegetables, including sugar snap peas, snow peas, asparagus, green beans, and peas. Put the vegetables in a large salad bowl and add 8 oz finely sliced smoked salmon, 1 finely diced red onion, 2 tablespoons chopped parsley, 1 cup watercress, and 2 tablespoons olive oil. Season to taste with salt and pepper and mix lightly. In a small bowl make a lemon yogurt dressing by beating together 4 tablespoons plain yogurt, the zest and juice of 1 lemon, 2 tablespoons chopped dill, 2 tablespoons olive oil, and salt and pepper. Drizzle the dressing over the salad and serve.

white bean, feta, & pepper salad

Serves **4**

Preparation time **15 minutes, plus cooling**

Cooking time **10–15 minutes**

2 **red bell peppers**, halved, cored, and seeded

4 tablespoons **olive oil**

2 tablespoons **balsamic vinegar** or **red wine vinegar**

3 teaspoons **sundried tomato paste**

4 teaspoons **capers**

2 x 13¼ oz cans **cannellini beans** or **navy beans** or **chickpeas**

½ **red onion**, finely chopped

4 **celery sticks**, sliced

4 oz **feta cheese**

1 **romaine lettuce**

salt and **pepper**

Put the peppers, skin side up, on a foil-lined broiler rack. Brush them with a little of the oil and cook under a preheated broiler for 10–12 minutes or until they are softened and the skins charred. Put the peppers in a plastic bag, fold over the top to seal and allow to cool.

Meanwhile, make the dressing by mixing the remaining oil with the vinegar, tomato paste, and chopped capers. Season to taste with salt and pepper.

Rinse and drain the beans or chickpeas. Stir them into the dressing with the onion and celery.

Peel the skins off the peppers and cut the flesh into strips. Add to the beans and gently toss together. Crumble the feta cheese over the top and serve the salad on a bed of lettuce leaves.

For white bean, feta, & chorizo salad, prepare the salad as above. Cut 3 chorizo sausages into slices and fry them in a large, nonstick skillet over a high heat until crispy and golden. Remove them from the pan and drain on paper towels, reserving the oil in the pan. Add 1 finely diced red onion to the pan and cook for 2 minutes over a low heat. Deglaze the pan with 3 tablespoons vinegar. Pour over the salad and toss to combine. Garnish with 4 oz crumbled feta and serve immediately.

puy lentil salad & salsa verde

Serves **4**
Preparation time **15 minutes**
Cooking time **45 minutes**

1 teaspoon **olive oil**
1 small **onion**, finely chopped
1½ cups **Puy lentils**
2 cups **vegetable stock**
7 oz **cherry tomatoes**, chopped
bunch of **scallions**, finely sliced

Salsa verde
4 tablespoons chopped **mixed herbs**, such as **parsley, cilantro,** and **chives**
1 tablespoon **capers**, drained
2 **anchovy fillets** (optional)
1 tablespoon **olive oil**
grated **zest** and **juice** of 1 **lime**

Heat the oil in a saucepan, add the onion, and fry for 2–3 minutes until it is beginning to soften.

Add the lentils and stock, bring to a boil, then cover and simmer for 30–40 minutes until the lentils are tender and the stock has been absorbed. Add the tomatoes and scallions to the lentils. Stir well to mix.

Meanwhile, make the salsa by putting the herbs, capers, anchovies (if used), oil, and lime zest and juice in a food processor and whizzing for a few seconds until combined but still retaining a little texture.

Drizzle the salsa over the warm lentils and toss together. Serve with toasted chapattis or flat breads.

For lentil salad with lamb koftas, prepare the lentil salad as above, but using a mixture of 3 tablespoons olive oil and 2 tablespoons chopped mint for the dressing. Mix 13 oz ground lamb with 1 teaspoon red pepper flakes and 1 finely diced red onion. Chop a small bunch of mint and add it to the mixture with 1½ teaspoons ground cumin. Season to taste with salt and pepper. Take a small handful of the mixture and push it onto a metal or presoaked wooden skewer. Repeat until all the mixture is used. Cook the skewers on a barbecue or under a preheated medium broiler, turning occasionally, for 6 minutes or until cooked through. Serve the koftas with the lentil salad and a dollop of Greek or whole milk yogurt.

farfalle, tomato, & pesto salad

Serves **4–6**
Preparation time **10 minutes**
Cooking time **20 minutes**

13 oz **farfalle pasta**
5 tablespoons **basil pesto**
  (see below)
2 cups **arugula**
4 oz **sun-blushed tomatoes**
small handful of **basil leaves**
½ cup **Parmesan cheese**,
  grated
salt and **pepper**

Cook the pasta in a large saucepan of boiling water for about 10 minutes or according to the instructions on the package until it is just tender. Refresh under cold water, drain, and place in a large salad bowl. Stir in the pesto so that the pasta is well coated and add the arugula.

Drain the tomatoes and add them to the pasta with the basil leaves and three-quarters of the grated Parmesan. Season with salt and pepper, and serve the salad sprinkled with the remaining Parmesan.

For basil pesto, to serve with the above salad, separate a large bunch of basil and put the leaves in a food processor or blender with 3 tablespoons toasted pine nuts, 1 small chopped garlic clove, and 6 tablespoons grated Parmesan cheese. Whiz until just combined then drizzle in 4–5 tablespoons of olive oil to make a smooth paste. Cover the pesto with a layer of olive oil and keep in the refrigerator for up to 7 days.

wild rice & turkey salad

Serves **4**

Preparation time **10 minutes**, plus cooling

Cooking time **30 minutes**

1½ cups **wild rice**

2 **green apples**, finely sliced

¾ cup **pecan nuts**

zest and **juice** of 2 **oranges**

½ cup **dried cranberries**

3 tablespoons **olive oil**

2 tablespoons chopped **parsley**

4 **turkey fillets**, each about 4 oz

salt and **pepper**

Cook the rice according to the instructions on the package and allow to cool to room temperature.

Mix the apples into the rice with the pecans, the orange zest and juice, and the cranberries. Season to taste with salt and pepper.

Mix together the oil and parsley. Cut the turkey fillets into halves or thirds lengthwise and cover with this mixture. Heat a skillet until it is hot but not smoking and cook the turkey for 2 minutes on each side. Slice the turkey, arrange the pieces next to the rice salad, and serve immediately.

For sticky citrus pork chops with wild rice salad, beat the zest and juice of 1 orange, 2 tablespoons orange marmalade, 1 tablespoon soy sauce, and 1 tablespoon sweet chili sauce. Heat a large skillet over a high heat and seal 4 pork chops, each about 6 oz, for 2 minutes on each side. Put the chops on a foil-lined baking sheet and cover with the marinade. Cook in a preheated oven, 350°F, for 10–15 minutes until cooked through. Prepare the salad as above and serve topped with the pork chops.

pasta, crab, & arugula salad

Serves **1**
Preparation time **5 minutes,**
  plus cooling
Cooking time **10 minutes**

2 oz **dried pasta**, such as
  rigatoni
grated **zest** and **juice** of
  ½ **lime**
2 tablespoons **sour cream**
3¼ oz can **crabmeat**, drained
8 **cherry tomatoes**, halved
handful of **arugula**

Cook the pasta according to the instructions on the package and allow to cool.

Mix together the lime zest and juice, sour cream, and crabmeat in a large bowl. Add the cooled pasta and mix again.

Add the tomatoes to the bowl with the arugula, toss everything together, and serve.

For pasta salad with tuna & chili, cook the pasta as above. Drain a 4½ oz can tuna and mix through the cooked pasta. Seed and finely chop 1 red chili and add to the pasta with the zest and juice of 1 lemon, 2 tablespoons chopped parsley, a handful of arugula leaves, and 2 tablespoons olive oil. Season to taste with salt and pepper and serve.

puy lentils, salmon, & dill salad

Serves **4**

Preparation time **30 minutes,
    plus cooking and chilling**

Cooking time **35–40 minutes**

1 lb **salmon fillet**
2 tablespoons **dry white wine**
4 **red bell peppers**, halved
    and seeded
1¾ cups **Puy lentils**
large handful of **dill**, chopped
1 bunch of **scallions**, finely
    sliced
lemon juice, for squeezing
pepper

Dressing
2 **green chilies**, seeded and
    chopped
large handful of **flat-leaf
    parsley**, chopped
large handful of **dill**, chopped
2 **garlic cloves**
1 teaspoon **Dijon mustard**
8 tablespoons **lemon juice**
1 tablespoon **olive oil**

Put the salmon on a sheet of foil and spoon over the wine. Gather up the foil and fold over at the top to seal. Place on a baking sheet and bake in a preheated oven, 400°F, for 15–20 minutes until cooked. Allow to cool, then flake, cover, and chill.

Broil the peppers and peel away the skins following the instructions on page 174. Reserve the pepper juices.

Make the dressing. Whiz the chilies, parsley, dill, garlic, mustard, and lemon juice in a food processor until smooth. With the motor running, drizzle in the oil until the mixture is thick.

Put the lentils in a large saucepan with plenty of water, bring to a boil, then simmer gently for 15–20 minutes until cooked but still firm to the bite. Drain them and place in a bowl with the red peppers and their juice. Add all the dill and most of the scallions. Season with pepper to taste.

Stir the dressing into the hot lentils and allow to infuse. To serve, top the lentils with the flaked salmon and gently mix through the lentils and dressing. Add a little lemon juice and the remaining scallions.

For salmon salad & crushed potatoes, boil 13 oz new potatoes for 15–20 minutes. Drain and cool slightly, then lightly crush. Mix in 4 tablespoons olive oil, 2 tablespoons small capers, 1 bunch sliced scallions, and salt and pepper. Prepare the salmon as above and flake it through the potatoes. Add a handful of chopped dill and 2 cups watercress. Serve with lemon and olive oil.

bulghur wheat salad

Serves **4–6**
Preparation time **15 minutes**,
  plus soaking

¾ cup **bulghur wheat**
13 oz **cherry tomatoes**, diced
6 **scallions**, finely chopped
bunch of **parsley**, chopped
small bunch of **mint**, chopped
salt and **pepper**

Dressing
¼ teaspoon **allspice**
¼ teaspoon **cinnamon**
juice of 1 **lemon**
4 tablespoons **olive oil**

Put the bulghur wheat in a bowl and cover with cold water. Allow to stand for at least 1 hour.

Meanwhile, make the dressing by beating together the allspice, cinnamon, lemon juice, and oil.

Strain the bulghur wheat through a fine sieve and leave to stand for 5 minutes, squeezing out as much water as possible. Add the tomatoes, scallions, parsley, and mint to the bulghur wheat. Add the dressing and mix well. Season with salt and pepper to taste. Leaving the salad in the refrigerator for a few hours will intensify the flavors.

For bulghur wheat salad with whole broiled snapper, score the snapper 3 times diagonally on each side. Mix together 1 teaspoon ground cumin, ¼ teaspoon turmeric, 1 teaspoon ground ginger, 1 teaspoon ground chili, the zest and juice of 1 lemon, and 2 tablespoons olive oil. Put lemon slices inside the fish and rub them with the spice mixture. Put the fish under a low broiler and cook for 20–25 minutes, turning halfway through cooking, until opaque but still juicy. Put the bulghur wheat salad on a large serving plate, arrange the broiled snapper on top, and serve.

mushroom & ricotta pasta salad

Serves **4–6**
Preparation time **20 minutes**
Cooking time **12 minutes**

1 cup **ricotta cheese**
2 tablespoons chopped
  parsley
2 tablespoons chopped
  rosemary
2 tablespoons chopped
  thyme
2 tablespoons chopped **basil**
¾ cup finely grated
  Parmesan cheese
13 oz **penne pasta**
2 tablespoons **olive oil**
1 lb mixed **mushrooms**,
  including **chestnut** and
  portobello
1 **garlic clove**, crushed
salt and **pepper**

Mix the ricotta with the herbs and Parmesan in a small bowl and season to taste with salt and pepper.

Cook the pasta in a large saucepan of boiling water for 10 minutes or according to the instructions on the package until it is just tender.

Meanwhile, slice the mushrooms. Heat the oil in a large skillet over a high heat and fry the mushrooms for 1 minute. Add the crushed garlic, season with salt and pepper, and cook for 2 minutes.

Drain the cooked pasta, add the mushrooms and stir through. Add the ricotta mixture and mix well. Serve with more chopped herbs and Parmesan, if desired.

For pancetta & creamy mushroom pasta, cut 7 oz pancetta into small batons and fry until crispy. Add to the cooked pasta together with the mushrooms. Stir through 2 cups baby spinach and serve.

corn, tomato, & black bean salad

Serves **4**

Preparation time **10 minutes**

Cooking time **10 minutes**

4 **corn ears**, leaves and fibers removed

8 oz **cherry tomatoes**, halved

13 oz can **black beans**, drained and rinsed

1 **red onion**, finely diced

1 **avocado**, peeled, pitted, and diced

small bunch of **cilantro**, roughly chopped

Dressing

juice of 1 **lime**

2 tablespoons **canola oil**

2–3 drops **Tabasco sauce**

Cook the corn ears in boiling water for 7–10 minutes. Cool briefly under running cold water then scrape off the kernels with a knife. Put the kernels in a large bowl with the tomatoes, black beans, onion, and avocado and mix with the cilantro.

Make the dressing by mixing together the lime juice, oil, and Tabasco.

Drizzle the dressing over the salad, stir carefully to combine, and serve immediately.

For chili shrimp with corn & black bean salad,

finely chop 2 garlic cloves and seed and finely chop 2 long red chilies. Heat 1½ tablespoons vegetable oil in a wok or large skillet over a high heat and cook 24 peeled and butterflied shrimp with the tails on. Stir-fry for 1 minute, then add the garlic and chilies. Fry for an additional 2 minutes until just cooked through. Turn off the heat and stir through 3 tablespoons chopped cilantro. Serve the shrimp over the corn and black bean salad garnished with extra cilantro leaves and lime wedges.

chickpea & herb salad

Serves **4**

Preparation time **10 minutes, plus cooling**

Cooking time **10 minutes**

½ cup **bulghur wheat**

4 tablespoons **olive oil**

1 tablespoon **lemon juice**

2 tablespoons chopped **flat-leaf parsley**

1 tablespoon chopped **mint**

13 oz can **chickpeas**, drained and rinsed

4 oz **cherry tomatoes**, halved

1 tablespoon chopped **mild onion**

½ **cucumber**

5 oz **feta cheese**

salt and **pepper**

Put the bulghur wheat in a heatproof bowl and pour over sufficient boiling water just to cover. Set aside until the water has been absorbed. If you want to give a fluffier finish to the bulghur wheat, transfer it to a steamer and steam for 5 minutes. Spread on a plate to cool.

Mix together the olive oil, lemon juice, parsley, and mint in a large salad bowl. Season to taste with salt and pepper. Add the chickpeas, tomatoes, onion, and bulghur wheat.

Dice the cucumber and add to the bowl. Mix well and add the diced feta, stirring lightly to avoid breaking up the cheese. Serve immediately.

For beet & chickpea salad, combine 3 cups baby chard with 13 oz rinsed and drained canned chickpeas, 1 cup precooked and diced beets in a large mixing bowl. Cut an orange in half and put the halves on a hot griddle pan until golden and not black. Squeeze the juice into a small bowl and add 1 teaspoon honey and 3 tablespoons olive oil. Beat together, then dress the salad lightly and crumble over 5 oz feta.

chickpea & cherry tomato salad

Serves **4**

Preparation time **15 minutes**,
  plus soaking and cooling

Cooking time **1–1½ hours**

1½ cups **dried chickpeas**

13 oz **cherry tomatoes**,
  halved

4 **celery sticks**, sliced

4 **scallions**, sliced

⅓ cup **Kalamata olives**

Mint and **Yogurt Dressing**
  (see page 15)

black pepper

mint leaves, to garnish

Soak the chickpeas overnight in cold water. Drain the chickpeas, rinse well, and drain again. Put them into a large saucepan, cover with plenty of cold water and bring to a boil. Simmer for 1–1½ hours or according to the instructions on the package until cooked and soft. Add extra water if necessary. Drain and allow to cool.

Put the tomatoes, celery, scallions, olives, and chickpeas into a large serving bowl and mix well. Stir in the dressing, season with black pepper, garnish with mint leaves, and serve.

For chickpea salad with harissa lamb, marinate

12 lamb chops in 3 tablespoons harissa paste mixed with 2 tablespoons olive oil. Allow the lamb to marinate for at least 1 hour, preferably overnight. Prepare the chickpea salad as above. Heat a large griddle pan and fry the lamb in batches for 2–3 minutes on each side until just cooked through and still pink in the middle. Remove and allow to rest for 5 minutes. Serve with the salad, drizzled with the Mint & Yogurt Dressing and some roughly chopped mint.

risoni, sweet potato, & bacon salad

Serves **4–6**
Preparation time **20 minutes**
Cooking time **30 minutes**

2 large **sweet potatoes**,
   peeled and cut into small
   dice
2 tablespoons **olive oil**, plus
   extra for drizzling
7 oz **bacon**
8 oz **risoni** or **orzo pasta**
1⅓ cups frozen **peas**
4 oz **feta cheese**
small bunch of **mint**, chopped
salt and **pepper**

Put the sweet potatoes on a large baking sheet and drizzle with olive oil and salt and pepper. Bake in a preheated oven, 375°F, for 20–25 minutes until just cooked through.

Finely slice the bacon. Heat a large skillet over a high heat and fry the bacon for 4 minutes until golden and crispy. Drain on paper towels and reserve.

Meanwhile, cook the pasta in a large saucepan of boiling water for 10 minutes or according to the instructions on the package. Add the peas and cook for 2 more minutes and drain.

Remove the sweet potatoes from the oven and mix with the pasta and peas. Add the bacon and crumble over the feta, reserving some of both for garnish. Add 2 tablespoons olive oil and the chopped mint and combine well. Garnish with the reserved bacon and feta and serve.

For cajun chicken & risoni salad, drizzle 2 boneless, skinless chicken breasts with olive oil and sprinkle with 2 tablespoons cajun seasoning. Heat a skillet and fry the chicken for 5 minutes on either side until cooked through. Thinly slice the chicken and serve with the risoni salad as above.

fruit salads

mixed berry salad

Serves **4–6**
Preparation time **10 minutes**

2⅔ cups **strawberries**
2 cups **raspberries**
1½ cups **blueberries**
1 cup **blackberries**
small bunch of **mint**, finely
    chopped, a few sprigs
    reserved for decoration
3 tablespoons **elderflower
    syrup**

Hull and halve the strawberries. Wash all the berries and drain well.

Add the chopped mint to the berries with the elderflower syrup, mix carefully, and serve, decorated with the reserved mint sprigs.

For warm berry salad, dilute 6 tablespoons elderflower syrup in 2½ cups water, add ¼ cup superfine sugar and bring to a boil in a heavy saucepan. Add 2⅔ cups strawberries, 2 cups raspberries, 1½ cups blueberries, and 1 cup blackberries, prepared as above, to the pan and turn off the heat. Let the berries cool slightly, then serve with vanilla ice cream. The berries will keep for up to 5 days in the syrup in the refrigerator.

exotic fruit salad

Serves **6–8**
Preparation time **10 minutes**

1 large ripe **pineapple**,
  about 3 lb
1 **papaya**, about 13 oz
3 **passion fruit**
juice of 1 **lime**
mint sprigs, to decorate

Peel and core the pineapple and cut the flesh into small wedges. Do the same with the papaya, carefully removing the seeds with a spoon. Put the pineapple and papaya in a serving bowl.

Cut the passion fruit in half and scrape the pulp into the bowl. Add the lime juice, mix carefully, and serve decorated with mint sprigs.

For grilled pineapple with lime sugar, peel a 3 lb pineapple and cut it into quarters, removing the core. Cut each quarter into 4 long pieces and thread them onto metal or presoaked wooden skewers. Put the zest of 3 limes into a food processor and add ⅔ cup granulated sugar. Whiz briefly then spread the sugar on a baking sheet and allow to dry for at least 1 hour. Heat a griddle pan to a medium heat and cook the pineapple for 2 minutes on each side until golden and caramelized. Sprinkle with the lime sugar and serve. Store unused lime sugar in a dry, airtight container.

citrus salad

Serves **4–6**

Preparation time **15–20 minutes**, plus marinating

Cooking time **5 minutes**

2 **oranges**
2 **satsumas**
2 **limes**
4 **blood oranges**
1 **ruby grapefruit**
⅔ cup **superfine sugar**
⅔ cup **water**

Remove the rind from the 2 oranges and the 2 limes using a zester. Peel all the fruit with a knife, carefully removing all the pith. Slice the oranges and satsumas and segment the limes, blood oranges, and grapefruit.

Reserve some of the orange and lime rind for decoration and put the rest into a saucepan with the sugar and water. Cook over a gentle heat, stirring until the sugar has dissolved. Pour the syrup over the fruit and let stand in the refrigerator for at least 1 hour before serving. Serve decorated with the reserved orange and lime rind.

For Grand Marnier citrus sauce, to serve with citrus salad, mix ½ cup superfine sugar, the juice and rind of 2 oranges, and ¼ cup water in a small, heavy saucepan. Bring to a boil, then turn the heat to low and reduce the liquid by two-thirds until syrupy. Once the correct consistency is reached, add 3 tablespoons Grand Marnier, pour over the citrus salad, and serve.

rhubarb & strawberry salad

Serves **4**
Preparation time **20 minutes**
Cooking time **20 minutes**

1 lb **rhubarb**
½ cup **superfine sugar**
⅔ cup **water**
1 **vanilla bean**
2 teaspoons **rose water**
2⅔ cups **strawberries**

To serve
mascarpone cheese or
  Greek yogurt
6 tablespoons roughly
  chopped **pistachio nuts**

Cut the rhubarb into 1½ inch lengths and put them in a shallow, nonmetallic ovenproof dish.

Put the sugar and water in a small saucepan over a low heat and stir until the sugar has dissolved. Add the vanilla bean and rose water. Pour the syrup over the rhubarb, cover with foil, and bake in a preheated oven, 350°F, for 12–15 minutes until just soft.

Meanwhile, hull and halve the strawberries. When the rhubarb is cooked, discard the vanilla bean and add the strawberries, cover, and allow to stand for 5 minutes. Transfer the fruit to serving plates, spoon some of the cooking liquid over each one and add a dollop of mascarpone or yogurt and a sprinkling of chopped pistachios.

For rhubarb, apple, & scallop salad, prepare 1 lb rhubarb as above but add only ⅓ cup sugar. Cut an apple into matchsticks and combine in a bowl with the rhubarb, 2 cups watercress, and 1 sliced avocado. Heat 1 tablespoon vegetable oil in a skillet over a high heat and fry 12 large scallops for 2 minutes on each side until just cooked through. Remove and keep warm. Toss the salad with 1 tablespoon white balsamic vinegar, 2 tablespoons olive oil, and salt and pepper. Arrange the scallops on top of the salad and serve.

spiced fruit salad

Serves **6**
Preparation time **15 minutes**,
  plus cooling and chilling
Cooking time **2 minutes**

1 **vanilla bean**, plus extra for
  decorating if desired
2½ tablespoons **superfine
  sugar**
¾ cup **water**
1 **hot red chili**
4 **clementines**
2 **peaches**
½ **cantaloupe melon**
1½ cups **blueberries**

Use the tip of a small, sharp knife to score the vanilla bean lengthwise through to the center. Put the sugar and water in a saucepan and heat gently until the sugar dissolves. Halve and seed the chili and add it to the saucepan with the vanilla bean. Heat gently for 2 minutes, then remove the pan from the heat and allow the syrup to cool.

Cut away the rind from the clementines and slice the flesh. Remove the pits from the peaches and slice the flesh. Seed the melon and cut the flesh into small chunks, discarding the skin.

Mix the fruits in a serving dish and pour over the warm syrup, discarding the chili and vanilla bean. Allow the syrup to cool completely, then cover the fruit salad and chill until you are ready to serve. Serve decorated with a vanilla bean, if desired.

For spiced fruit salad syrup, to serve with the above fruit salad, add to the syrup 1 lemon grass stalk cut in half and bruised with a meat tenderizer, 3 kaffir lime leaves and ¾ inch fresh ginger root peeled and roughly sliced. Add these with the chili and prepare in the same way.

poached fruit with ginger cookies

Serves **6–8**
Preparation time **15 minutes**
Cooking time **20 minutes**

1 cup **superfine sugar**
10 cups **water**
1 **vanilla bean**, plus extra for
   decorating if desired
4 **peaches**
4 **nectarines**
10 **apricots**

To serve
mascarpone cheese
3 **ginger cookies**, crushed

Put the sugar, water, and vanilla bean in a large, heavy saucepan and heat gently, stirring, until the sugar has dissolved. Bring to a low simmer, add the fruit, and cover with a circle of waxed or parchment paper to hold the fruit in the syrup. Simmer for 2 minutes then turn off the heat and allow to cool.

Remove the fruit from the liquid with a slotted spoon, reserving the poaching liquid. Peel the skins from the fruit, then cut them in half and remove the pits.

Put 1 cup of the poaching liquid in a small, heavy saucepan and heat to reduce it for 6–8 minutes until it has a syrupy consistency. Put the fruit in a large bowl, pour over the syrup, and toss gently. Arrange the fruit on serving plates, add a spoonful of mascarpone to each one, and sprinkle with crushed ginger cookies. Serve decorated with a vanilla bean, if desired.

For poached stone fruit with raspberry coulis,

put 1¼ cups frozen raspberries and 3 tablespoons superfine sugar in a heavy saucepan. Slowly bring up to a boil, stirring, to dissolve the sugar. Simmer for 2–3 minutes until the coulis has a syrupy consistency. Remove from the heat and strain through a fine sieve. Poach the stone fruit as above and serve with the raspberry coulis and a drizzle of custard.

mixed fruit salad

Serves **6–8**
Preparation time **15 minutes**

¼ **watermelon**
½ **cantaloupe melon**
1 **mango**
2 **green apples**
2 **bananas**
3 **kiwifruit**
1⅓ cups **strawberries**
1½ cups **blueberries**

Peel and seed both the melons and cut the flesh into 1 inch chunks. Put them in a large bowl. Peel and dice the mango, dice the apples, and slice the bananas. Add to the bowl with the melon.

Peel the kiwifruit and cut the flesh into rounds, add to the bowl along with the berries, and mix the fruit together carefully.

For exotic fruit salad with passion fruit cream, beat together 4 tablespoons mascarpone cheese, ¾ cup heavy cream, and 2 tablespoons sifted confectioners' sugar in a bowl until soft peaks form. Gently fold in the pulp of 2 passion fruit. Serve a spoonful with the exotic fruit salad.

cherries with cinnamon crumble

Serves **4–6**
Preparation time **15 minutes**,
   plus cooling
Cooking time **20 minutes**

6 cups pitted **cherries**
1 cup **superfine sugar**
1¾ cups **water**
1 **vanilla bean**
2 **cloves**
strips of **orange peel**,
   to decorate

Crumble
2 oz **fruit loaf**
½ tablespoon **unsalted butter**
⅛ teaspoon **cinnamon**
1 tablespoon **superfine sugar**

Cinnamon cream
1 tablespoon **confectioners'**
   sugar
⅔ cup **whipping cream**
¼ teaspoon **cinnamon**

Put the cherries in a large bowl. Place the sugar in a heavy saucepan and add the water, vanilla bean, cloves, and orange peel. Bring to a boil, stirring occasionally, then pour the syrup over the cherries. Allow to cool.

Make the crumble. Cut the fruit loaf into ½ inch dice. Melt the butter and drizzle it over the fruit loaf. Mix together the cinnamon and sugar and sprinkle over the fruit loaf. Mix well, transfer to a baking sheet, and cook in a preheated oven, 375°F, for 4–5 minutes until golden and crunchy. Remove the crumble from the oven and allow to cool.

Meanwhile, make the cinnamon cream. Sift the confectioners' sugar over the cream, add the cinnamon, and beat until firm peaks form.

Serve the cherries with a small amount of syrup, a spoonful of the cinnamon cream, and a sprinkling of the fruit loaf crumble. Decorate with strips of orange peel.

For chocolate & cinnamon sauce, to serve with the cherries, combine ½ cup chopped bittersweet chocolate (use chocolate with 70 percent cocoa solids), 1 tablespoon butter, ½ cup cream, and ½ teaspoon ground cinnamon in a small, heavy saucepan over a low heat. Stir the sauce until all the chocolate has melted and it is smooth and glossy. Turn off the heat and reserve. Prepare the cherries as above and serve with a drizzle of the chocolate cinnamon sauce.

winter fruit salad

Serves **4–6**
Preparation time **5 minutes**
Cooking time **30 minutes**

⅔ cup **prunes**, pitted
⅔ cup ready-to-eat **dried peaches**
⅔ cup ready-to-eat **dried pears**
⅔ cup ready-to-eat **dried apples**
⅔ cup ready-to-eat **dried apricots**
⅓ cup ready-to-eat **dried figs**
1 **cinnamon stick**
4 **cloves**
zest of 1 **lemon**
¼ cup **superfine sugar**

To serve
Greek or **whole milk yogurt**
honey

Put the prunes and the ready-to-eat dried fruits, the cinnamon stick, cloves, lemon zest, and sugar in a saucepan and cover with cold water. Set over a medium heat and simmer for 15 minutes until the fruit plumps up.

Remove the pan from the heat and strain the fruits, reserving the liquid and discarding the cinnamon stick. Return the liquid to the heat for 10 minutes until reduced.

Return the fruits to the syrup, warm them through and serve with yogurt and a drizzle of honey.

For roasted winter fruit salad, core and quarter 3 pears and 3 apples and put them in an ovenproof dish. Halve and pit 3 plums and add them to the dish with ⅓ cup dried figs, ½ cup frozen cranberries, a cinnamon stick, and 4 cloves. Dot the fruit with ¼ cup unsalted butter, then sprinkle with ¼ cup brown sugar. Bake in a preheated oven, 350°F, for 20 minutes until soft. Serve with yogurt and honey.

fruit salad with lemon grass syrup

Serves **4–6**

Preparation time **10 minutes**, plus cooling

Cooking time **10 minutes**

½ inch **fresh ginger root**, peeled and sliced

1 **lemon grass stalk**, lightly bruised

½ cup **superfine sugar**

⅔ cup **water**

2 **papayas**, peeled and seeded

2 **mangoes**, peeled and pitted

2 **guavas**, peeled and pitted

10 **litchis**, peeled

2 tablespoons **toasted coconut**

Put the ginger, lemon grass, sugar, and water into a small, heavy saucepan and simmer for 5 minutes. Remove from the heat and allow to cool.

Cut the papaya flesh into long wedges and put them in a bowl. Cut the mangoes and guavas into small wedges and add to the papaya with the litchis. Add 3 tablespoons of the syrup and combine carefully.

Transfer the salad to serving dishes, drizzle over some of the remaining syrup, and sprinkle with the toasted coconut.

For toasted coconut, to decorate the fruit salad, break open a coconut, drain away the juice and peel off the outer tough husk. Run a vegetable peeler along the broken edge of the coconut. Once you have enough shavings, lay them flat on a baking sheet and toast in a preheated oven, 400°F, for 3–4 minutes until golden brown.

chargrilled fruit with chili salt

Serves **6–8**
Preparation time **15 minutes**
Cooking time **10 minutes**

1 large **mango**, peeled and
   pitted
½ **pineapple**, peeled
2 **bananas**
½ teaspoon **dried red pepper
   flakes**
1 tablespoon **sea salt** or
   vanilla sea salt

Cut the mango into ¾ inch pieces and cut the
pineapple into small wedges. Cut the bananas into
thick slices. Skewer the fruit onto metal or presoaked
wooden skewers, alternating the fruits.

Mix together the pepper flakes and salt and set aside.

Preheat a griddle pan to medium heat and grill the
skewers on each side for 3 minutes until golden and
caramelized. Remove the skewers from the heat,
sprinkle with the salt mix and serve.

For vanilla sea salt, to accompany chargrilled fruit
skewers, scrape the seeds of 1 vanilla bean into a
small bowl with 4 tablespoons sea salt. Stir to
combine well and allow to infuse for at least 2 hours.

papaya, lime, & almond salad

Serves **4**

Preparation time **15 minutes**, plus cooling

Cooking time **3–5 minutes**

3 firm, ripe **papayas**, peeled and seeded

2 **limes**

2 teaspoons **light brown sugar**

⅓ cup **toasted blanched almonds**

lime wedges, to decorate

Cut the papayas into large dice.

Finely grate the rind of both limes, then squeeze 1 of the limes and reserve the juice. Cut the pith off the second lime and segment the flesh over the bowl of diced papaya to catch the juice. Add the lime segments and grated zest to the papaya.

Pour the lime juice into a small saucepan with the sugar and heat gently until the sugar has dissolved. Remove from the heat and allow to cool.

Pour the cooled lime juice over the fruit and toss thoroughly. Add the toasted almonds and serve with lime wedges.

For papaya & lime salad with ginger granite, pour 4 cups ginger beer into a rectangular plastic container. Mix in 3 tablespoons chopped mint, put the container in the freezer, and leave for at least 4 hours. When the liquid is frozen scrape it with a fork until a fluffy ice has formed. Spoon the ice over the papaya and lime salad and serve immediately.

marsala poached pears

Serves **6**
Preparation time **10 minutes**
Cooking time **40 minutes**

1¼ cups **Marsala**
2 cups **red wine**
1 cup **superfine sugar**
2 tablespoons **lemon juice**
1 **cinnamon stick**
2 **star anise**
6 **pears**
clotted cream, to serve

Put the Marsala, red wine, sugar, lemon juice, the cinnamon stick and star anise in a heavy saucepan and bring to a low simmer.

Peel the pears, leaving the stalks in place, put them in the saucepan and cook for 20–25 minutes, turning occasionally, until they are soft. Remove the pears from the saucepan with a slotted spoon and set aside to cool.

Meanwhile, return the poaching liquid to the heat and boil to reduce for about 10 minutes until it is thick and syrupy. Serve the pears, drizzled with the syrup and accompanied by a spoonful of clotted cream.

For roasted pears with fudge sauce, halve 6 pears and remove the cores. Put the pears in an ovenproof dish and sprinkle with 5 tablespoons brown sugar and 1 teaspoon vanilla extract. Dot with 1½ tablespoons unsalted butter. Roast the pears in a preheated oven, 350°F, for 20 minutes until golden and soft. Meanwhile, combine ⅔ cup brown sugar, ½ cup cream, and 1½ tablespoons unsalted butter in a heavy saucepan, stirring until the sugar has dissolved. Simmer for 2 minutes then pour the sauce over the roasted pears and serve with a dollop of clotted cream.

melon & pineapple salad

Serves **4**

Preparation time **10 minutes**,
  plus standing

½ **cantaloupe melon**, peeled
  and seeded
½ small **pineapple**, peeled
grated **zest** of 1 **lime**
2 teaspoons **fructose**
lime slices, to decorate

Dice the melon and pineapple. Add the melon and pineapple to a bowl or plastic container.

Mix together the lime zest and fructose until well combined. Sprinkle this over the fruit and stir in well; in an hour or so the fructose will have dissolved. Decorate with the lime slices and serve.

For melon & pineapple salad with lime & ginger syrup, in a small, heavy saucepan combine ⅔ cup superfine sugar, ⅔ cup water, the zest and juice of 1 lime and ½ inch fresh ginger root, peeled and roughly sliced. Bring the mixture to a boil, stirring occasionally to dissolve the sugar. When the sugar has completely dissolved, remove the syrup from the heat, cover, and chill. Drizzle the syrup over the salad about 30 minutes before serving to allow the flavors to combine.

index

acknowledgments

Executive Editor: Nicola Hill
Editor: Charlotte Macey
Executive Art Editor: Leigh Jones
Designer: Jo Tapper
Photographer: Lis Parsons
Home Economist: Sunil Vijayaker
Props Stylist: Liz Hippisley
Production Manager: Carolin Stransky

Special photography: © Octopus Publishing Group Limited/Lis Parsons
Other photography: © Octopus Publishing Group Limited 55, 79, 101, 121, 139, 161, 173, 175, 179, 183, 185, 201, 231, 234; /Jeremy Hopley 39, 51; /Dave Jordan 159; /William Lingwood 59, 63, 89, 93, 96, 117, 127, 167, 203; /Peter Myers 45; /William Reavell 193; /Gareth Sambridge 151, 191, 217; /Phillip Webb 105.